STAFF AND EDUCATIONAL DEVELOPMENT ASSOCIATION

Peer Assessment in Practice

By

Sally Brown

SEDA Paper 102
April 1998
ISBN 0 946815 99 2

Contents

Page

Introduction   5
Sally Brown, University of Northumbria at Newcastle

Involving Students in Feedback and Assessment   9
Nancy Falchikov, Napier University, Edinburgh

Assessing Using Peer Review   23
Keith Pond, Loughborough University & Rehan ul-Haq, University of Birmingham

Peer Assessment: Report of a Project involving group presentations   45
and assessment by peers
Carole Mindham, Manchester Metropolitan University

Lessons from coming of age in Peer Assessment and Group Work   67
Hazel Fullerton & Yacub Rafiq, University of Plymouth

Peer Assessment: Lessons and Pitfalls   79
Leonora Ritter, Charles Sturt University

Peer Assessment - A Construction "Tool"?   87
W D Sher & D R Twigg, Loughborough University

What do Students think about Assessment?   107
Sally Brown, Kay Sambell, Liz McDowell,
University of Northumbria at Newcastle

Practical Pointers on Peer Assessment   113
Phil Race, University of Durham

Introduction

As assessment becomes increasingly diversified in Higher Education worldwide, more and more students are finding that they can no longer expect to sit back and leave the work of assessment to their tutors. Whether they become involved in **grading** each others work on the basis of correct solutions provided by tutors, or whether they become fully involved in making detailed **summative judgements** which contribute to final marks, students are increasingly being required to play their part in a process that was formerly the domain primarily of academic staff.

Involving students in Peer assessment is nothing new. In a forerunner to this publication, SCED paper number 63, *Self and Peer Assessment,* published in 1991 but now out of print, described a number of examples of the use of peer assessment in UK institutions, and the practice at this time had been established in several of the institutions described for some years. At that time, however, there was a positively evangelical air about this and a number of other publications that extolled the virtues of peer assessment somewhat uncritically.

This edited collection, comprising seven chapters, takes a more sober view perhaps. It has been specifically put together to reflect the actual experiences of a number of Higher Education teachers who have been using peer assessment with their students over a period of time and who have discovered not only the advantages associated, but also the pitfalls and problems that can be part of the process. The express purpose of this SEDA paper is to offer the benefit of the contributors experiences to others who may be about to embark on the use of peer assessment or who perhaps are looking for ways of doing it better.

In the first chapter, Nancy Falchikov, who has been writing about peer assessment for at least ten years and who many regard as a seminal influence in the field, describes the outcomes of her involvement in the Assessment Strategies in Scottish Higher Education (ASSHE) project. This surveyed innovative assessment practice across Scotland's institutions of Higher Education between 1995 and 1996 . Here in a chapter entitled **Involving Students in Feedback and Assessment** she writes about the methods by which students are involved in assessing themselves and each other and explores some of the reported benefits and problems associated with student involvement, as well as some of the factors that are likely to help or hinder success in implementation.

The next five chapters describe peer assessment in practice in a number of institutions. The first of these is by Keith Pond and Rehan Ul Haq writing on **Assessing Using Peer review**: As they put it, they are interested in adopting the learning benefits of peer review and mitigating the potential learning disbenefits of pure peer assessment through effective assessment design and structure. They describe, warts and all, how peer assessment has worked for them at Loughborough University, and offer some suggestions on how to do it better.

Next Carole Mindham writes on **Peer assessment: A Report of a Project Involving Group Presentations and Assessment by Peers**. She describes the use of peer assessment in the Education Faculty of Manchester Metropolitan University by students working in groups on presentations concerned with Schools radio or television programmes. Her experiences have led her to believe that the process is not without difficulties, but is worth continuing with, under conditions of progressive improvement.

Following on from this, Hazel Fullerton and Yacub Rafiq describe in **Lessons From Coming of Age in Peer Assessment in Group Work** their experiences of using peer assessment for group work at Plymouth University, interspersing their account with a commentary on what they have learnt as the process has matured in practice. Learning from experience forms the basis of the next chapter also: Leonora Ritter describes **in Peer Assessment: Lessons and Pitfalls** how she rejected earlier less successful models of peer assessment, going on to introduce peer assessment of essays on two courses in History of Childhood and Australian Studies History at the Charles Sturt University in Australia. Her pragmatic account provides learning points for others on making peer assessment work well.

The penultimate chapter, based on the Impact of Innovative Assessment Project at the University of Northumbria at Newcastle, asks **What do Students Think about Peer Assessment?** The chapter quotes extensively from our research, providing comments in the students' own words about what is necessary to make peer assessment a practical alternative to traditional assessment .Our findings suggest that students do gain benefit from being involved in peer assessment, so long as they are fully briefed and the process is well organised and effectively designed.

The last chapter, by Phil Race offers some **Practical Pointers on Peer Assessment**. He begins by rehearsing the reasons why we might wish to use peer assessment and provides some suggestions about what kinds of assessment contexts are suitable for the implementation of peer assessment. A central section of the chapter takes the reader through a step-by-step process of devising criteria as a negotiated process with students, and he concludes with some suggestions on how to get the most out of the peer assessment process.

Peer assessment is here to stay. The benefits as described by the contributors here make it apparent that the involvement of students in assessing each other is extremely valuable in terms of learning gain, as well as making assessment much more fully integrated into the whole process of teaching and learning. We have a responsibility to ensure that students develop their powers of evaluation and judgement, and a good way to do this is through becoming involved in peer assessment. To be successful in so doing, they need guidance and support from those who teach them and this collection aims to help this to be done well.

References

Brown S and Dove P (1991) Self and Peer assessment,) SCED Paper number 63, SCED (now the Staff and Educational Development Association, SEDA)

Involving students in feed-back and assessment

A report from the Assessment Strategies in Scottish Higher Education (ASSHE) project

Nancy Falchikov
Napier University, Edinburgh

Abstract

This paper begins by considering the methods by which we may involve students in the assessment process. Self and peer assessment is then examined in relation to Atkins et al's (1993) current ideas about the four main purposes of higher education. The changes to assessment which have involved students in Scotland that were highlighted by the recent Assessment Strategies in Scottish Higher Education (ASSHE) survey are then reviewed. A number of issues are addressed:

- Where are self and peer assessments reported to be taking place?

- What is the nature of student involvement in assessment?

- Levels and varieties of student involvement

- What is being assessed by students?

- Students and feedback

- By what means are self and peer assessments being carried out?

- What is the rationale given for involving students in assessment?

- Perceived or measured benefits of student involvement

- Problems encountered when involving students in assessment

- Which factors helped get the initiative off the ground?

- Factors contributing to the longer term success of initiatives

- Hindering factors

Introduction

Student involvement in the assessment process typically takes the form of self assessment, peer assessment or collaborative assessment. In self assessment, students are required to rate their own performance, while in peer assessment they rate the performance of their peers. Self and peer assessment may also include some degree of collaboration between lecturers and students, depending on whether, how, and to what extent the criteria of assessment and other dimensions of the process are discussed and agreed by both parties. Many studies of self or peer assessment report benefits in terms of enhancements of student learning (e.g. Falchikov, 1986, 1988; Boud, 1988). Boud (1986) has argued that "the development of skills in self assessment lies at the core of higher education", and that we, as teachers, should be finding "whatever opportunities we can to promote self assessment in the courses we teach" (1986, p. 1). However, it has also been argued that interdependence precedes independence (Bruffee, 1993). Thus, it seems that peer assessment may also aid in the development of good self assessment skills.

In the past, all decisions regarding students were made by the lecturer. Curriculum design and content, mode of course delivery, timing and type of assessments were all determined by the teacher. Thus, power over learning, as well as power over ultimate certification of students, resided with the teacher. This situation continues in many parts of higher education today. However, a common theme in the most recent studies involving self and peer assessment world-wide seems to be a growing awareness on the part of teachers of the need to increase the participation of students in the learning process, and to develop a less teacher-centred education. This trend is, paradoxically, accompanied by statements on the part of some politicians, urging teachers to return to their traditional positions of power and authority in the classroom.

The mechanics of self and peer assessment

Methods of implementing self assessment have been elaborated by researchers (e.g. Boud, 1986). Similarly, several case studies of peer assessment provide enough information to enable interested readers to set up schemes of their own (e.g. Falchikov, 1988; Goldfinch and Raeside, 1990; Mathews, 1994 and other chapters in this volume). Two factors appear to influence the success of schemes which involve students. They are:

1. Thorough preparation for the exercise
2. Valuing the exercise

Whether students are being required to assess their own work or that of their peers, it is essential that the criteria by which the work will be judged are made explicit, and that the preparation for the exercise is done thoroughly. If students are also involved in the process of identifying criteria, it is likely that they will feel a greater degree of ownership of them than would be the case otherwise. Any one who has involved their students in assessment will know that self and peer assessment is hard work. Students are being asked to spend time and energy on the exercise, and staff are required to ensure the organisation and smooth running of the scheme. A good outcome in terms of improved student learning is likely to be more easily achieved if class time is made available for the reflection necessary for successful self and peer assessment, and if the marks generated by students are not routinely "over-ruled" in favour of staff marks on completion of the exercise. However, there may be potential problems if student generated marks "count" towards important grading. (See Boud, 1989).

How self and peer assessment relate to current ideas about the purposes of higher education

Atkins et al (1993) see higher education as having a multiplicity of purposes. They suggest four key objectives to take it into the twenty first century. Higher education, they argue, should provide:

1. A general educational experience
2. Preparation for knowledge creation, dissemination and application
3. Specific vocational preparation (usually linked to entry to a profession)
4. Preparation for general employment.

Involving students in assessment may be seen to serve all of these purposes to a greater or lesser degree. For example, the ability to think critically and conceptually, and to recognise the relativity of knowledge and biases in the assumptions of one's self and of others must be aided by exposure to work and ideas other than one's own and by other aspects of self and peer assessment. Preparation for knowledge creation, dissemination and application requires an understanding of the methodologies and procedures necessary for these activities. Involving students in assessment, where much of the process must be demystified and made explicit, may, thus, be seen as central to the achievement of this purpose of higher education. Specific vocational or professional preparation involves "integration of relevant theoretical knowledge with knowledge of processes and principles developed from analysis of practice (self and others) (Atkins et al, 1993, p. 28). Atkins et al also argue that, in the context of preparation for specific vocational or professional employment, "assessment should require demonstration of the process of skills of being a reflective practitioner (including self assessment and analysis of development needs)" (p. 30). Similarly, Laurillard (1993) argues that education in general "must act at the second-order level of 'reflecting on' experience" (p. 26). Preparation for general employment also requires the ability to carry out self and peer assessments (e.g. Hughes and Large, 1993). The Enterprise in Higher Education (EHE) initiative which places great value on personal transferable skills has also been cited as a new rationale for the involvement of students in assessment in the 1990s.

The ASSHE project: recent changes to assessment which involve students

The Assessment Strategies in Scottish Higher Education (ASSHE) project aimed to identify evolving assessment practices in all Scottish higher education institutions, and to document and analyse these changes. Data collection, by means of self-completion of a pro forma, began in 1995 and the database was closed in mid-1996. Information concerning any change in assessment was sought: changes in what is being assessed, in how students are assessed, in the place and timing of assessments, and in who is involved in assessing students' work. In all, well over 300 initiatives were reported. Information supplied by colleagues throughout Scotland relating to changes in assessment practices suggested that involvement of students in assessment and feedback provision is widespread. Nearly a third of database entries reported that students were involved at some stage of assessment.

Where are self and peer assessments reported to be taking place?

Changes to assessment practices which involve students appear to occur in a wide variety of areas of higher education across Scotland. These are shown in figure 1.

Distribution and peer assessment and student feedback initiatives in Scottish higher education

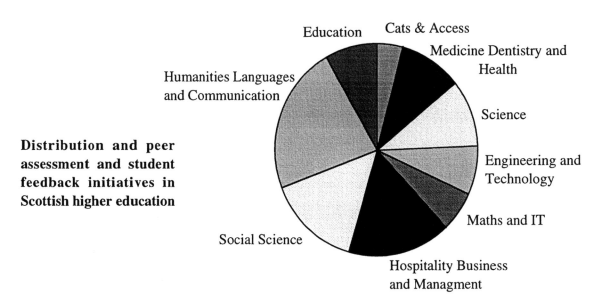

Figure 1

What is the nature of student involvement in assessment?

Many Scottish students are now involved in assessment in a variety of ways: self assessment, peer assessment, feedback provision and negotiation or collaboration with lecturers concerning some aspect of the process. Most frequently occurring student involvement is by means of peer assessment, usually in the context of group work and/or the provision of feedback.

Levels and varieties of student involvement

Levels of student involvement reported varied from a single simple decision regarding some aspect of assessment, such as choice of submission date or mode of assessment, to involvement in the entire assessment process. In some schemes, students also provided grades which counted as part of the summative assessment.

In some studies reported, the emphasis was on the provision of feedback rather than of a mark. These studies also ranged from the simple to the complex, from the formal to the informal and from formative to summative.

What is being assessed by students?

Educational products and processes, and the acquisition of professional skills were all found to be the focus of student assessment schemes in Scotland.

Assessment of products
Products which have been assessed in part or whole by students may be classified into four groups: written; visual; oral; professional. In the first group of "written products", essays, examinations, tests, exercises, experimental write-ups and reports occurred relatively frequently. In addition, there were a few less usual products such as case studies, group diaries and business plans which are being assessed by students. Students are involved in the assessment of "visual products" such as posters and video films, and personal art, design and architectural design. Oral presentations and seminars have been classified as products in cases where the performance is assessed as a finished product by the student audience. Finally, products associated with future professional practice such as open learning packs and other teaching materials constituted the fourth category of product.

Assessment of processes
The assessment of the contribution of individuals to the production of many of these products also involved students. In other words, students were often involved in the assessment of processes. Processes were categorised into three types:

- "Contribution to the production of ..." an educational product, often a group project report
- "Group process analysis" in which students were required to identify the "qualities and competencies of group members" rather than estimate their overall contribution
- "Individual", a very small category in which experiential learning in the workplace was self assessed by the learner.

Assessment of professional skills
The assessments of clinical skills in a variety of medical and para-medical disciplines in Scotland now involve students, as do assessments of skills in computer programming, interviewing skills and legal skills. Teaching performances of both trainees preparing for the teaching profession and "regular" students engaging in peer teaching are also reported to involve self or peer assessment.

Students appear to be involved in the assessment of products about twice as frequently as in the assessment of processes. Assessments of professional skills occur less frequently.

Students and feedback

Many students in a variety of settings appear to be receiving formative feedback from their peers: students of hospitality and tourism, business and management studies students, health science and nursing students, students of literary theory, geography, psychology, biology and chemistry. Feedback features prominently in more than a quarter of the examples of student involvement in assessment. Students either receive structured feedback from tutors or themselves provide feedback to their peers. This practice may be informal and without structure, or more formally structured. My own use of Peer Feedback Marking (PFM) (Falchikov, 1995a; 1995b; 1994) and peer criticism (Falchikov, 1996) involves students in the provision of constructive feedback to their peers. The practice of PFM requires the identification, by students and tutor, of strengths of presentations and the provision of suggestions for improvement. Where peer criticism occurs, student written work is reviewed by a peer and this formative feedback used by the author in second and third drafts. Evaluations of these studies indicated that students found the feedback useful, that student generated feedback compared favourably with that generated by tutors and that students appeared to have acted on some advice given.

By what means are self and peer assessments being carried out?

In a large number of initiatives reported to the ASSHE team, student assessors used forms, checklists, marking schemes or marking bands or criteria which had been supplied by the lecturer. An equally large number indicated that students had been involved in discussions with lecturers concerning criteria of assessment, or had derived these criteria or dimensions of assessment for themselves. Thus, in the majority of cases where students are involved in assessment in Scottish higher education, there are mechanisms for "making visible the invisible" in terms of what is required of them. Many students now do not need to infer or guess the rules of the game: the criteria are made known and stated explicitly. What is the rationale given for involving students in assessment?

Reasons given for introducing self or peer assessment, or for involving students in the provision of feedback were varied, though the majority concerned an improvement in learning and assessment. (See figure 2).

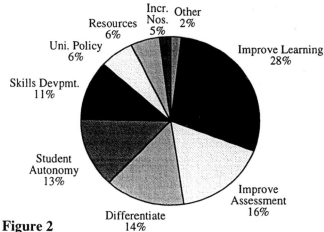

Rationales for involving students in assessment

Figure 2

Most frequently occurring rationale was to improve student learning in some way (28.0% of the total). Several lecturers who submitted entries to the database wished to increase the depth, intensity or quality of student thinking by means of the initiatives they described. The second most frequently mentioned reason for involving students in assessment was to improve assessment practices more generally. The third most frequently mentioned reason for involving students, in peer assessment in this case, was in order to differentiate between students working together in a group. Some teachers wished to devolve power and responsibility to students, and saw self or peer assessment as a means to this end. Thus, the fourth most frequently mentioned reason was to increase student autonomy and responsibility. Next most popular reason for involving students in assessment was to improve their skills development. University policy or external stimuli contributed only 6.4% of reasons for introducing an initiative. For one lecturer, the change was prompted by circumstances familiar to us all: "Module numbers rocketed" .... "so peer assessment was the obvious choice. In a few cases, staff had involved students in assessment to save time in marking. In at least one case the "hoped for reduction in time spent on assessment by staff" was not achieved, but the initiative was retained as other beneficial features had been identified.

Perceived or measured benefits of student involvement

The benefits of student involvement in the assessment process have been reported in several studies prior to the present survey (e.g. Fineman, 1981; Earl, 1986; Falchikov, 1986; Fox, 1989), and these findings are amply supported by information supplied by contributors to the ASSHE database. All Scottish teachers who reported recent changes to assessment were also asked to identify benefits and problems associated with their initiative. Almost all contributors identified at least one benefit to students, and a very large number of benefits were recorded in total. A slightly smaller number of benefits to staff were listed, though this category was also very large.

Benefits to students
Most frequently mentioned benefit of participating in assessment for students was that of skills development. High on the list of skills were those of group working. The development of interpersonal skills was also mentioned by lecturers, in addition to development of personal transferable skills, organisational skills and listening skills. Student involvement in assessment which provided speedy and useful feedback to large numbers of students was also rated as particularly beneficial. Staff perceived that "more", "speedy", "improved", "incremental" "wide ranging" feedback allowed students "to moderate their behaviour and improve performance". Student involvement in assessment was also seen to increase student autonomy and independence, and encourage students to take responsibility for their own learning. Similarly, student involvement, enthusiasm and motivation were reported by some Scottish teachers as improving as a result of participation in some aspect of assessment. Other colleagues discovered for themselves that student "ownership" of some part or parts of the process is beneficial. Several teachers reported increases in student confidence, as well as increases in understanding, reflection and intellectual development. Other teachers valued the increase in control experienced by students who participate in assessment.

Benefits to staff

Benefits to staff who involve their students in assessment also appeared to be plentiful and varied. Most frequently identified benefit concerned professional practice and the quality of teaching. Teachers welcomed the increased opportunities to monitor student progress and identify potential problems afforded by student involvement in assessment. Other benefits reported by lecturers related to improvements in the marking system, while yet others involved improved relationships with students and clearer insights into what it is to be a student today. While the change of role required of the teacher when moving from traditional to more student centred learning is often difficult, a few colleagues identified this change as a benefit to them. One contributor enjoyed "learning from students". The involvement of students in assessment seems to have given rise to satisfaction to some teachers who found the initiative stimulating, interesting and fun.

As we can see, teachers perceive there to be a wealth of benefits associated with involving students in assessment. Some of these conclusions appear to be based on feedback from students involved, or from direct observation of student cohorts. However, some staff perceptions of student benefits suggested that "what I perceive to be good for you must be beneficial", and a parallel direct measure of student perceptions would be of great interest and value. For example, "increased autonomy" is listed by some teachers as a benefit to students. While most readers of this chapter might well agree that this is, indeed, a desirable feature of any scheme, many students, and some colleagues, would not agree. As one contributor pointed out, "In a way, this kind of assessment is a belief system, (which) penetrates deeply into ways of working and learning. Similarly, Banta et al's (1996) survey of changing assessment practices in the USA made frequent reference to the importance of the philosophy of learning and assessment of individuals, groups, departments or the academic community.

Problems encountered when involving students in assessment

Problems encountered when involving students in assessment affect both students and staff. The ASSHE survey suggested that many problems affecting students seem to be related to peer assessment and working in groups. The main problem for students seems to be their reluctance to participate in schemes and their lack of experience in so doing. However, these problems appear to be short lived. All lecturers who identified this as a problem qualified it.
e.g.

> *"Initially there was some resistance to change, but there are no problems now."*
> *"Student uncertainty in the early stages ..."*

Any one who has involved their students in assessment will know that some students dislike assessing or judging their peers. This, too, was the experience of Scottish colleagues. Group composition and dynamics were also found to contribute to student reluctance to participate in group activities. One contributor identified "character conflicts" as a problem, while others listed "backsliders", "the one student who does not participate" and "quiet students who end up in groups with low motivation".

Both students and staff found that peer assessment can be time consuming. The majority of contributors, however, felt that the time, spent by both themselves and students, was well spent.

Which factors helped get the initiative off the ground?

Factors identified by contributors to the database as "helping to get the initiative off the ground" fell into a number of categories. (See figure 3)

Factors supporting initiatives

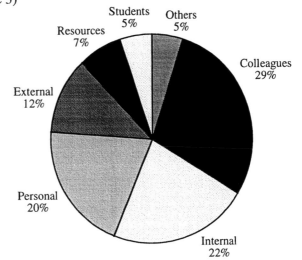

Figure 3

Nearly a third of the entries detailing assessment initiatives which involve students mentioned colleagues within their department or university more widely as a major influence, and it seems that colleagues are likely to be influential whatever the nature of the change being attempted. Characteristics of supportive colleagues identified by the survey included:

- commitment to improve student learning
- shared philosophy
- commitment to the initiative itself
- a good working relationship
- support
- enthusiasm
- energy
- hard work

Given the importance of one's colleagues, it is unfortunate that we do not always have the opportunity to choose them ourselves! Similarly, less immediate colleagues in the form of Heads of Department, Heads of School, Departmental Steering Committees, Curriculum Development Committees and "individual senior managers", in addition to University policy were also listed as being influential. Next in importance in terms of launching an initiative were personal factors such as expertise, knowledge, commitment, enthusiasm and interests. Encouragement from sources external to the university or college, such as external examiners, also seemed to play a part in getting several initiatives off the ground. In addition, "comments on assessment by Scottish

Higher Education Funding Council (SHEFC)" and "Scottish Office Education Department (SOED)'s introduction of national teaching competencies" were deemed important for both stimulus to, and implementation of, change.

Factors contributing to the longer term success of initiatives

Contributors to the database identified many factors which helped get their initiatives off the ground, as we have seen above. However, as many of these initiatives were in their infancy when records were received, we have a less clear idea about what might contribute to longer term success. However, those initiatives which have been "running" for longer periods, and the results of a similar assessment project in the United States, provide some clues as to factors which might contribute to continuing success. Two features Scottish teachers identified as important in introducing change, namely, support from within the institution and enthusiastic dedicated colleagues, also featured prominently as contributing to longer term success in the similar survey of changes in assessment practices in America (Banta et al, 1996). There are other similarities between the two studies. Benefits to students and staff appear to play an important part in the continued success of initiatives as well as in their implementation. Banta et al's (1996) survey also pointed to the importance of a shared philosophy for the success of an initiative. Contributors to the American survey identified "faculty culture" and "shared concerns" as important factors in accounting for success, and see the "building of cultural expectations", and the aligning of student and staff goals as crucial to this end. Reports of some more established Scottish and some American initiatives also described staff (or faculty) "ownership" as a factor contributing to success. The importance of the pilot study is identified by some colleagues in Scotland, while, in the American study, methodology more generally is seen as important. The same argument may be applied to the importance of evaluation, and "having the curricular changes validated by ongoing collection of data" (Magruder and Young, in Banda et al, 1996, p. 170). Funding and the provision of resources contribute to success - on both sides of the Atlantic. However, it is only in the USA that some teachers are reported to be in receipt of "small stipends" for participating in initiatives (Cohen et al, in Banda et al, 1996, p. 222). An important element of "success" is the extent to which initiatives are taken up by others. Again, we have yet to see the longer term impact of the ASSHE survey in this respect. Banta et al's contributors identified both internal dissemination activities such as newsletters and staff development workshops or seminars and external activities such as conferences as important in ensuring more enduring success.

Hindering factors

Reports to the ASSHE project supplied some clues concerning what may be described as "hindering factors" to the involvement of students in the assessment process. These appear to occur in three linked areas: the teacher, the student and the institution. Teacher factors seem to involve traditional conceptions of student and teacher roles, in which teachers "run the show", and students receive the benefits of teacher experience rather than of their own. Involving students in important processes such as assessment requires a change in the traditional teacher (and student) role. Moreover, any change is stressful and upsetting. Many teachers may be unaware of the benefits of involving students in assessment. Others need to be convinced of its reliability, and, reasonably, demand evidence. Fortunately, such evidence now exists, and peer assessment, for example, is regarded as a reliable indicator of performance (e.g. Magin, 1993a; 1993b). Similarly, we know how to maximise the benefits and reliability of self assessment (e.g. Falchikov and Boud, 1989; Boud and Falchikov, 1989).

Student factors in some ways resemble teacher factors, in that traditional conceptions of what students and teachers "ought to do" are sometimes involved. Students are also concerned with the reliability of the system.

Finally, the institution itself may hinder the wider involvement of students in assessment. Some teachers in Scottish higher education reported difficulties of introducing self or peer assessment into the system formally, due to over rigid and bureaucratic central mechanisms for change. Some changes are occurring, however, which have been stimulated by bodies outside the university such as external examiners and recommendations from Teaching Quality Assessors. While issues of quality are clearly important to those in senior and administrative positions in higher education institutions, their concerns about reliability often echo those of teachers and students.

Conclusion

The ASSHE survey has provided us with a wealth of useful information concerning many issues regarding changes to assessment practices. Pressure for change in assessment in Scottish higher education appears to come from several directions (c.f. Nightingale et al's (1996) report on innovative assessment practices in Australia). As in Australia, pressure for change in Scotland also appears to come from a desire to move away from a conception of assessment as a simple measure of the amount of knowledge a student has, by broadening the range of what is assessed. Further pressure for change comes from the desire, "to harness the full power of assessment and feedback in support of learning" (Nightingale et al, 1996, p. 6). Improvements to student learning occupied a prominent place on the agenda of many contributors to the ASSHE database. In addition, many teachers now share the belief that higher education should actively encourage the development of students' abilities to evaluate their own work and that of their peers. Such abilities can be cultivated only by involving students in assessment. While the practice of involving students is clearly not without its problems, it is important to remember that lecturer marking is itself far from a perfect art, with recent reports (e.g. Newstead and Dennis, 1994) finding gross discrepancies between marks awarded by very experienced markers. The logic of the position where reliability of marks increases with the number of markers involved (student or staff) (e.g. Houston et al, 1991), is that we should welcome opportunities to involve students in assessment. Moreover, the benefits, of involving students in well planned and executed assessment schemes, in terms of enhanced learning and personal and intellectual development, provides further impetus to such changes. Of course, it is possible that some schemes have been implemented in response to increased class sizes or other situational demands, without knowledge of the wealth of theory supporting such initiatives and the benefits to be derived from them. However, for once, it is good that an act of expediency appears to be bringing benefits to students.

References

Atkins, M.J, Beattie, J. and Dockrell, W.B. (1993) Assessment issues in higher education. Employment Department, Further & Higher Education Branch: London

Banta, T.W., Lund, J.P., Black, K. and Oblander, F.W. (1996) Assessment in practice, Jossey-Bass: San Francisco

Boud, D. (1989) The role of self-assessment in student grading, Assessment and Evaluation in Higher Education, 14, 20-30

Boud, D. (Ed.) (1988) Developing student autonomy in learning (2nd. ed.), Kogan Page: London & New York

Boud, D. (1986) Implementing student self-assessment, HERDSA Green Guide No. 5, University of New South Wales: Sydney

Boud, D. and Falchikov, N. (1989) Quantitative studies of student self-assessment in higher education: a critical analysis of findings, Higher Education, 18, 529-549

Bruffee, K.A. (1993) Collaborative Learning. Higher education, interdependence, and the authority of knowledge. The Johns Hopkins University Press: Baltimore and London.

Cohen, S., Chechile, R.A. and Smith, G.E. (1996) A detailed, multi site evaluation of curricular software, in Banta, T.W., Lund, J.P., Black, K. and Oblander, F.W. (1996) Assessment in practice, Jossey-Bass: San Francisco, 220-222

Earl, S.E. (1986) Staff and peer assessment - measuring an individual's contribution to group performance, Assessment and Evaluation in Higher Education, 11(1), 60-69

Falchikov, N. (1996) "Improving learning through critical peer feedback and reflection", Higher Education Research and Development, 19, 214- 218

Falchikov, N. (1995a) Peer Feedback Marking: developing peer assessment, Innovations in Education and Training International, 32(2), 175-187

Falchikov, N. (1995b) "Improving feedback to and from students", in Towards better learning: assessment for learning in higher education, (Ed. Peter Knight), Kogan Page: London

Falchikov, N. (1994) "Learning from peer feedback marking: student and teacher perspectives, in Group and interactive learning, Foot, H.C., Howe, C.J., Anderson, A., Tolmie, A.K. & Warden, D.A. (Eds.), Computational Mechanics Publications: Southampton and Boston

Falchikov, N. (1988) Self and peer assessment of a group project designed to promote the skills of capability, Programmed Learning and Educational Technology, 25 (4), 327-339.

Involving students in feedback and assessment

Falchikov, N. (1986) Product comparisons and process benefits of collaborative self and peer group assessments, Assessment and Evaluation in Higher Education, 11(2), 146-166.

Falchikov, N. & Boud, D. (1989) Student Self-Assessment in Higher Education: a meta-analysis, Review of Educational Research, 59 (4), 395-430

Fineman, S. (1981) Reflections on peer teaching and peer assessment - an undergraduate experience, Assessment and Evaluation in Higher Education, 6(1), 82-93

Fox, D. (1989) Peer assessment of an essay assignment, HERDSA News, 11(2), 6-7

Goldfinch, J. and Raeside, R. (1990) Development of a peer assessment technique for obtaining marks on a group project, Assessment and Evaluation in Higher Education, 15(3), 210-231

Houston, W., Raymond, M. & Svec, J. (1991) Adjustment for rater effects in performance assessment. Applied Psychological Measurement, 15 (4), pp. 409-421.

Hughes, I.E. and Large, B.J. (1993) Staff and peer-group assessment of oral communication skills, Studies in Higher Education, 18(3), 379-385

Laurillard, D. (1993) Rethinking University Teaching, Routledge: London and New York

Magin, D. (1993a) Evaluating peer marking procedures for assessing communication and group process skills: two case studies. Paper presented at the Pacific Rim Symposium on Higher Education. Hilo, Hawaii, June 2-5.

Magin, D. (1993b) Should student peer ratings be used as part of summative assessment? Research and Development in Higher Education, 16, pp. 537-542.

Magruder, W.J. and Young, C.C. (1996) Value-added talent development in general education, in Banta, T.W., Lund, J.P., Black, K. and Oblander, F.W. (1996) Assessment in practice, Jossey-Bass: San Francisco, 169-171

Mathews, B.P. (1994) Assessing individual contributions: experience of peer evaluation in major group projects, British Journal of Educational Technology, 25(1), 19-28

Newstead, S. and Dennis, I. (1994) Examiners examined: the reliability of exam marking in psychology. The Psychologist, 7 (5), 216-219

Nightingale, P., Te White, I., Toohey, S., Ryan, G., Hughes, C. and Magin, D. (1996), Assessing learning in universities, University of New South Wales Press: Sydney

Assessing using peer review

Adopting the learning benefits of peer review and mitigating the potential learning disbenefits of pure peer assessment through design and structure

Keith Pond, Loughborough University
Rehan ul-Haq, The University of Birmingham

Summary

Our ongoing research, as reported in Pond, ul-Haq, (1994) and later in Pond, ul-Haq, Wade, (1995), has differentiated between Peer Review and Peer Assessment. We have identified the various benefits of the Peer Review process in enhancing the learning undertaken in tutorial sessions with undergraduates. Benefits include the utilisation of peer pressure in "out of class" group work activities, the exchange of ideas and giving presentations. In addition, we have identified the potential disbenefits of Peer Assessment where marking is influenced by motives of friendship or collusion or it can be dominated by individuals ("decibel" marking). The scope for weaker students to contribute little but benefit greatly from group efforts (parasites) was also seen. Drawbacks also include the increased administrative workload in setting up such a scheme.

This paper considers the 1995/96 implementation of the scheme and provides a tentative **blueprint** for future implementation.

Introduction

The 1995/96 academic year tutorial teaching structure on the BSc (Hons) Banking and Finance degree at Loughborough University Business School was developed on the premise that any Peer Assessment based system must be designed to encourage the positive aspects of this learning method and mitigate or discourage the negative aspects.

In 1995 we concluded our work into the learning benefits of Peer Review by stating that:

> *"the formal and informal feedback from students and the performance of sub-groups in tutorial sessions add weight to the contention that the Peer Review process improved learning outcomes and encouraged students to develop a deep learning approach to the subject. This could be further enhanced by student involvement in the assessment process too."*

> *(Pond, ul-Haq, Wade, 1995).*

Assessing using peer review

The Peer Review findings over the academic -years 1993/94 and 1994/95 have shown both a number of positive aspects of the Peer Review process in enhancing student learning and a number of negative effects of the same process which are further worsened by pure Peer Assessment.

This paper is based on a study that focuses on the enhancement of the quality of student learning in tutorials through the process of Peer Review, a process which borrows heavily from Peer Assessment. Brown and Knight (1994) stresses that "Peer Assessment is not a panacea for the problem of coping with increasing student numbers". Peer Review, however, focuses on the learning process rather than on the product. Saunders (1992) notes that "Students are being asked to ... evaluate their own strengths and weaknesses and to become aware of their personal as well as academic development." Students can, and do, use strategies, games and techniques to avoid making contributions (Lublin, 1987). This is counter-productive for learning.

It has been found that the use of peer and self-assessment may promote higher levels of thinking (Peer and Self-Assessment, Falchikov, 1991). In addition, Brown and Pendlebury (1992) argues that Peer Assessment "raises awareness of the importance of group dynamics as well as tasks in a group setting" (Brown, 1992). The student benefits of cooperative learning, critical ability, confidence and independence are all recognised as by-products of this process (Falchikov, 1991).

Staff can be reluctant to embark on Peer Assessment because of fears that "results may be unreliable", validating authorities may find the method unacceptable or students may feel resentful, (Habeshaw et al., 1993). Falchikov has shown, however, that Peer Assessments can be highly reliable and accurate (Falchikov, 1991). Brown and Dove offer anecdotal evidence of additional benefit from Peer Assessment. These include: ownership, motivation, autonomous learning and the development of transferable skills (Brown and Dove, 1991). Their paper also suggests that, in comparison to traditional tutorial and assessment methods Peer Assessment can be too demanding of students, too time consuming and criteria setting can be problematic.

The available evidence strongly suggests that Peer Review or Peer Assessment criteria should be clearly identified and made explicit. Students should not only understand what they are being assessed on but also the weighting of the criteria. Common problems with Peer

Assessment also had to be considered for this project. Relevant literature (Brown and Knight, 1994) and informal conversation with colleagues suggested that the following could often be observed:

- "Friendship marking", resulting in over-marking.

- "Collusive marking", resulting in a lack of differentiation within groups.

- "Decibel marking", where the noisiest get the highest marks.

- "Parasite marking", where students "piggy back" on group marks.

Assessing using peer review

By necessity Peer Review of process should be done by those involved in it (Brown and Knight, 1994). Any one, or a combination, of the above factors could invalidate peer generated marks, which could have serious consequences if they are used in the assessment of final grades. Indeed, the more important the level of the assessment, the more the above factors could come into play.

Figure 1, reviews the problems associated with pure Peer Assessment and the possible remedies suggested by the above literature and by the empirical evidence from the project itself.

| Problem | Possible Remedy | | | |
	A Ownership	B Justification	C Mark Responsibility	D Handout Preparation
Friendship Marking	√	√	√	
Collusive Marking	√		√	
Decibel (Leadership marking)	√	√		√
Parasite/Piggy-back marking	√	√		√
Sub-Group Domination in non-substantive roles	√			√

Key

A	Student Ownership of Assessment Criteria.
B	Evidence of Work Done to Justify Higher or Lower than Average Peer Allocated Points.
C	Responsibility for Determining the Final Mark Shared Between the Student and the Tutor.
D	Handout Preparation & Presentation on Rota Basis.

Figure 1. *Problems With Peer Review and Possible Remedies*

Student ownership of the assessment criteria was found to be fundamentally important. Evidence of the work done (or not done) when peers allocate a higher (or lower) than average point score was vital and the split responsibility for determining final marks between the students and the tutor was very helpful. In our scheme the students allocated the relative points share while the tutor determined the group average percentage marks. Additionally 3 certain tasks which could be dominated by stronger or more able individuals were allocated on an informal rota basis. (Appendix A sets out the modified Peer Review system used during the 1995/96 academic year). This allowed the Peer Review process to be more transparent and unburdened by the need to allocate final marks.

Peer Assessment, if designed, structured and used appropriately, has many positive benefits which can be used in appropriate situations to encourage learning, group interaction, critical review of relative performance and can engender increased responsibility for one's own learning.

Implementation of the scheme

In our 1993/94 implementation of Peer Review, we asked the students to set the assessment criteria. In 1994/95 the tutors set the criteria resulting in a noticeably large decrease in the ownership of the Peer Review/assessment process on the part of students. This resulted in lower student satisfaction ratings and, possibly, reduced learning benefits.

To mitigate these problems we reintroduced, in 1995/96, the setting of the modified Peer Review criteria by the students.

To generate understanding of the importance of the setting of assessment criteria, and to break the ice, we used the Clapping Game in an additional tutorial prior to the start of the presentation (see Figure 2).

An interactive group-based class activity to illustrate the importance of setting assessment criteria.

- Split the tutorial group into sub-groups.

- Select three volunteers to leave the room temporarily (explain that no harm will come to them).

- Tutor to explain that each volunteer will be asked to enter the room to clap.

- Clapper 1 enters, is instructed to clap for one minute, claps and sits down.

- Clapper 2 enters, is instructed to clap for one minute and is told that the clapping will be judged, claps and sits down. Discussion on qualities of clapping takes place.

- Clapper 3 enters and is instructed as before but is told that the clapping will be judged in terms of rhythm, movement, musicality, speed and volume.

- Clapper 3 claps and sits down.

- Whole group discusses "best" clapping performance.

- Whole group receives feedback from Clappers.

- Discussion on importance of criteria setting and knowledge of criteria ensues.

The normal conclusion is that knowledge of criteria improves performance.

Developed from an idea by Sally Brown (University of Northumbria).

Figure 2. *The "Clapping Game"*

Assessing using peer review

Criterion setting

Immediately after the Clapping Game, each sub-group was asked to discuss the key criteria by which they thought their work in the sub-groups, in and out of formal sessions, should be judged and to write these on flip-chart paper. The flip-chart sheets were then displayed on the walls and each sub-group rated the criteria in order of importance. A discussion of the criteria setting then took place with a consensus listing emerging. The tutorial members were asked not to discuss the Clapping Game or criteria setting with the other groups.

Once the Clapping Game and criteria setting process has been repeated for all the tutorial groups a final criteria list is drawn up:

- individual participation

- team spirit

- research/preparation

- contribution to tutorial.

1993/94 Criteria*	1994/95 Criteria**	1995/96 Criteria***
Input	Input	Individual Participation
Preparation	Preparation	Research/Preparation
Attendance	-	-
Share	-	-
Handout	-	-
Teamwork	Teamwork	Team Spirit
Presentation	-	-
-	-	Contribution to Tutorial

Note: * and*** Student generated and agreed, ** Tutor imposed.

Table 1. *Peer Review Criteria*

Table 1 shows that the criteria selected by the different methods (student versus tutor) over the three academic years were largely similar. Student feedback and attendance data indicate, however, that student-set criteria were the most effective in establishing ownership.

Implementing peer processes

The questions for the tutorials were set in advance distributed at a lecture in week 3. The tutor-selected sub-groups were instructed to use a rota system for the handout preparation and the presentation to mitigate the tendency for one student to dominate the sub-group by dominating these functions. In a tutorial session each sub-group presented its work and discussion followed.

Assessing using peer review

After the presentation and discussion each sub-group completed the Peer Review Rating Sheet (Appendix B) allocating a maximum of 16 points per student, being a maximum of 4 points per student per criteria. The tutor made a separate note of the percentage mark that reflected the quality and comprehensives of the sub-group's presentation. The design was based initially on work by Conway et al., (1993) and further developed by ourselves.

At the end of each tutorial the Peer Review Rating Sheets were collected in by the tutor and entered, on a weekly basis, into the Peer Review Marks Sheet spreadsheet (sample spreadsheet given in Appendix C). This spreadsheet was entered with the total points score from the Peer Review Rating Sheet per person per week, and the tutor given percentage mark per sub-group per week. Calculation of the individual sub-group member's weekly mark was effected by weighting the tutor-given mark in accordance with the Peer Review scores. (A sample of the formulae for the spreadsheet is given in Appendix D).

Whilst students were not given weekly individual percentage mark feedback, they were provided with the opportunity to see the tutor to obtain the same if they wished to do so. The peer-assessed component of the module was based on an average of the individual students' marks over five weeks.

The Standard Deviation (SD) of the sub-group marks provided by the spreadsheet indicated whether the sub-group members were marking each other's performance on a possible collusive basis (if SD < 0.5) or if a fair spread of marks were being given to differentiate between relative performances.

Week	6	7	8	9	10
Mean SD	0.527	0.887	0.645	0.717	0.774
High SD	0.908	1.500	1.600	1.299	1.299
Low SD	0.000	0.000	0.000	0.000	0.000

Table 2. *Mean, High, Low, Standard Deviation on Sub-Group Peer Review Marking,* (where SD < 0.5   Possible Collusive Marking)

The low SD in Table 2 seem to show that although some collusive marking may have occurred in specific sub-groups the mean SD in the marks clearly shows a non-collusive average whilst the high SD shows that a high level of differentiation between students, in the marks awarded, did take place.

In addition a SD for the Peer Review marks for individual students was also calculated on the spread sheet and is displayed in Table 3. These data show that students did discriminate between better and worse performing peers on a weekly basis. The lowest individual SD of 0.4 indicates that no student achieved identical assessments each week.

Mean SD	High SD	Low SD
0.654	1.939	0.400
	n (students) = < 1.	

Table 3. *Mean, High, Low Standard Deviations of Weekly Peer Generated Marks for Individual Students.*

Table 4 also shows the learning effect apparent in group activities. Collusive marking, shown by low SDs, appears to reduce as the module progresses.

As modified peer assessed tutorials make up 25% of the total module marks, the interim percentage marks would be divided by four to obtain the final contribution to the module grade.

Week	6	7	8	9	10	Total
Total Marks	7 groups 58%	5 groups 42%	6 groups 50%	6 groups 50%	4 groups 33%	28 groups 47% Average

Table 4. *Preparation of Sub-Groups with SD < 0.5, n (groups) 12 per week*

Although it would be dangerous and perhaps inaccurate to make direct and detailed comparison between findings in 1994/95 and 1995/96, due to the impact of semesterisation, the changes in the module and the unique assessment criteria generated or imposed in each year, the measurement of peer point variation is interesting. 1995/96 saw a clear reduction in groups where collusive marking (SD < 0.5) was observed. It is believed that this could be reduced further by peer point allocations being generated individually rather than by groups. It was felt, however, that the administrative burden of this would be magnified proportionately far more than the resultant benefit.

Leadership and domination

With regard to the issue of leadership or dominance we saw, during the 1995/96 academic year, that only four students had both an above sub-group average point score over the tutorial weeks and an SD in their marks of less than or equal to 0.5. This represented 7.8% of the total students and that only four groups (33.3%) were affected by this issue.

We concluded that there had been a reasonably low incidence of leadership or dominance. This had been a particular problem in the 1993194 academic year but has reduced substantially by the introduction of a rota system, during the 1994195 and 1995/96 academic year, for the preparation of handouts and the presentation.

Learning Outcomes and feedback

The mix of Peer Review, to enhance the learning benefits, and a controlled degree of limited Peer Assessment, to mitigate the disbenefits of traditional Peer Assessment, seems to have worked well. Initial results, as detailed above, show a increased ownership of the learning process and a reduced incidence of collusive marking and the problems of leadership and domination in the sub-groups.

As part of our assessment of the effectiveness of the tutorials we asked the students to complete the Peer Review Rating Sheet at the end of the Week 10 presentation tutorial and the forms were then collected.

Assessing using peer review

Question	Response Rate (n=51)	Mean Grading (range 1-5)	Min	Max	SD
1. Effectiveness of Peer Assessment for learning.	100.00%	4.08	2	5	0.81
2. Effectiveness of Peer Assessment for group work.	100.00%	4.16	2	5	0.67
3. Has Peer Assessment been useful?	100.00%	4.10	2	5	0.77
4. Continue to use?	100.00%	4.18	2	5	0.78
Q 1 to Q 3 Mean	100.00%	4.11			

Q's 1 to 3   5 = Very effective/useful
3 = Moderately effective/useful
1 = Not very effective/useful

Q4   5 = Must use again
3 = Perhaps use again
1 = Don't use again

Table 5. *Student Feedback Exercise, Summary of Peer Review Ratings*

The results of the student feedback exercise clearly show that students considered the Peer Review/ partial Peer Assessment exercise to be effective for learning, group work and to have been useful. The Mean Grading of 4.1 1 is derived after asking students to rank the level of their agreement with statements about the process on a 1 -> 5 scale. There was also clear agreement that this teaching method should continue to be used (Mean Grading - 4.18). Table 5 shows a complete breakdown of the feedback scores.

In addition 37 students included qualitative comments on the Peer Review Rating Sheet. The breakdown of the numbers of positive and negative responses detailed in Table 6 below.

Type of Response	Number of Responses	Percentage of Total
Positive	31	83.78
Negative	6	16.22
Total	37	100%

Note: n (sheets completed) = 37 out of n (total number of sheets completed with quantitative responses) = 51.

Table 6. *Breakdown of Positive and Negative Qualitative Responses on Peer Review Rating Sheet*

The positive comments included "Peer Assessment (sic) encourages you to do more preparation so that you gain better marks. Understanding of the topic is better through these tutorials", whilst not-positive comments focus on the study time taken in learning through such a method and the difficulties inherent in rating others' performance. Appendix E provides a full list of the comments received.

It is clear from the student responses that they found the Peer Review used here to be effective in enhancing their learning. With regard to the final academic arbiter of effectiveness, the examination results, it is not possible to state that the peer methodology directly and positively influenced the quality of examination results year on year due to the changes in the module structure. It is possible to say however that examination results were not worse than in previous years.

Future developments

The initial objective of this exercise in Peer Review was to identify the learning enhancement capability of the process and to determine whether full Peer Assessment, with the students awarding both the processual and summative marks, would be appropriate and feasible to use on this course at Loughborough University Business School.

Our research has both identified the positive learning benefits of Peer Review and the potential dis-benefits of Full Peer Assessment. In the 1995/96 implementation by combining processual Peer Review and tutor based summative assessment, we believe that we have found the best fit solution for our particular teaching and learning situation. Furthermore we propose to carry forward this method to the 1996/97 academic year and beyond.

Conclusion

The combination of Peer Review of non-classroom learning for tutorial presentations impacting on and adjusting tutor initiated summative marks seems, on the evidence available to us and presented above, to be an appropriate method for the learning needs of this cohort of students. This paper has documented the design and structure used by the authors.

Tutor Determined...Student Determined
"Traditional...Flexible Learning"
Tutor Assessment............................Peer Review.............................Peer Assessment

Figure 3. *The Assessment Style Continuum*

We acknowledge that tutor assessment, Peer Review only or full Peer Assessment methods may be more appropriate in other situations. This continuum of assessment styles, (see Figure 3) from tutor based, through some element of Peer Review to full student led Peer Assessment, provides a repertoire of assessment styles to match the requirements of a specific teaching and learning situation.

References

Brown, G. A. and Pendlebury, M. (1992) *Assessing Active Learning*, Sheffield: CVCP[USDU.

Brown, S. and Dove, P. (eds) (1991) *Self and Peer Assessment,* Birmingham, SCED Paper 63.

Brown, S. and Knight, P. (1994) 'Assessing Learners in Higher Education'. In Stephenson, J. (ed) *Teaching and Higher Education Series*, London: Kogan Page.

Conway, R. Kember, D., Sivan, A. and Wu M. (1993) 'Peer Assessment of an Individuals Contribution to a Group Project', *Assessment and Evaluation in Higher Education,* Vol 18, No 1.

Falchikov, N.(1991) Group Process Analysis. In Brown, S. and Dove, P.(eds) *Self and Peer Assessment*, Birmingham: SCED Paper 63.

Habeshaw, S., Gibbs, G. and Habeshaw, T. (1993) *53 Interesting Ways to Assess your Students*, Melksham: The Cromwell Press.

Lublin, J. (1987) 'Conducting Tutorials' Guide No 6, HERDSA.

Pond, K. and ul-Haq, R. (1994) Peer Review: *An Effective Method of Enhancing Student Learning in Tutorials*? Loughborough University Business School Research Series Paper 1994:11.

Pond, K. ul-Haq, R. and Wade, W. B. (1995) 'Peer Review - A Precursor to Peer Assessment', *Innovations in Education and Training International*, 32, 4, 314-323.

Pond, &, ul-Haq, R., (1996), *Assessing Using Peer Review*, Conference Paper -Northumbria Assessment Conference, University of Northumbria, Morpeth, Northumberland, 4-6th September 1996.

Saunders, D. (1992) 'Peer Tutoring in Higher Education', *Studies in Higher Education*, Vol 17, No. 2.

An earlier version of this paper was published under the title "Learning to Assess Students Using Peer Review" in Students in Education Evaluation Vol 23, No.4, pp331-348, 1997

Appendix A

Loughborough University
Business School

Tutorial Pack

Introduction to banking

		Page
Contents:	Tutorial Timetable	1
	Notes on Peer Assessment	2
	Coursework Assignment	6
	Tutorial Questions for Week 5	7
	Tutorial Questions for Week 6	10
	Tutorial Questions for Week 7	13
	Tutorial Questions for Week 8	15
	Tutorial Questions for Week 9	15
	Tutorial Questions for Week 10	22

Introduction to banking (BSA035)

Tutorials:

Tutorials will be based on role play exercises (weeks 4 and 11) or pre-circulated exercises, case studies and discussion topics. Students are expected to prepare for and participate in tutorials either individually or in groups as directed by their tutor.

The tutorials in weeks 6 to 10 inclusive will be assessed using Peer Assessment of group work. Precise details of the mechanics of this process will be given in week 3.

Method of Assessment:

1. Assessment of tutorial contribution - weeks 6 to 10 (25%)
2. Coursework (25%)
3. End of Semester test (50%)

Tutorial Schedule:

Wk	Tutorial topic	Comments
1	No tutorial	
2	No tutorial	
3	Tutorial and coursework briefing and Banking system	Coursework set
4	Lending propositions	Group Role Play
5	Lending criteria	Tutorial presentation
6	The Banker / Customer Relationship	Tutorial presentation*
7	Managing accounts / Closing accounts	Tutorial presentation* Coursework return
8	Managing accounts (esp. errors)	Tutorial presentation*
9	The collecting banker	Tutorial presentation*
10	The paying banker	Tutorial presentation*
11	Securities	Group Role Play Coursework return
12	No tutorial	

* Peer Assessed tutorials - marks count towards end of semester assessment (25%)

Introduction to banking
Week 6 to 10 assessed tutorials - semester 1

1.   Peer Review

Peer Review is all about taking responsibility for your own learning. It is not a new technique in education and it has been shown to have significant advantages for all students. Linked with group or team work Peer Review helps to develop a critical awareness of strengths and weaknesses in others as well as in oneself.

As you work in sub-groups you will see clearly just how much each sub-group member contributes to the sub-group effort and output. Whilst the tutor will award the group mark each week only YOU know how well each individual sub-group member has contributed. Each week you will be asked to complete a simple form to indicate each member's contribution in respect of various predetermined criteria. A blank PEER REVIEW RATING FORM is reproduced in this tutorial pack. The criteria against which contributions will be reviewed will be devised by YOU.

2.   Tutorials - The Mechanics

Within tutorial groups "sub-groups" will be established to prepare answers to designated questions for each week of tutorials. The "sub-groups" will be selected randomly and you may find yourself working with people you have never spoken to before - this should ensure that, as well as improving banking knowledge, team - working skills are developed.

Each week the "sub-groups" are expected to:

1.   Produce a handout summarising their answer to the question set.
       Handouts should not exceed 1 A4 side but need not be typed.

2.   Arrange (via July Bowley or Joyce Tuson in the Banking Centre) for 12 (fourteen) copies of
       the handout to be made, These will be distributed at the tutorial.

3.   Be prepared to give a 5 to 20 minute presentation of the answer to the designated question.

4.   Be prepared to answer questions from other tutorial group members on its question.

5.   Be prepared to ask questions about other groups' presentations.

6.   Prepare answers (to be discussed in tutorial) for the short answer questions.

       AND FINALLY

7.   complete a PEER REVIEW RATING FORM in respect of the "sub-group" members'
       individual contributions to the group effort.

3.   **Allocation of Questions**

Week Sub-Group	6	7	8	9	10
A	ql	ql	ql	ql	ql
B	q2	q2	q2	q2	q2
C	q3	q3	q3	q3	q3

Each sub-group should also prepare answers to all of the short answer questions on the tutorial sheet.

4.   **Allocation of Marks**

Student determined Peer Review gradings will be used to indicate the share of the tutor awarded mark awarded to each individual group member.

The tutor awarded sub-group mark for each presentation will take into consideration the following: content of answer, understanding of problem, practicality of response, handout and presentation quality. The most important of these criteria will be the first two.

5.   **Conclusion**

These measures will encourage groups to work together and develop team - working, presentation and critical review skills and, in so doing, enhance the learning environment in tutorial sessions. Tutorials will be focused and individual students will benefit by learning from peers, obtaining constructive feedback on their own work and by leaving the tutorial with handouts and notes relating to all tutorial questions.

Loughborough University Business School

Peer assessed introduction to banking tutorials

Peer review rating sheet

Instructions:

1. Peer Assessment rating relates ONLY to your group's discussions before and during the tutorial;

2. Insert a contribution rating for each criteria for each group member using the following key:

4	Very significant contribution*
3	Major contribution
2	Satisfactory (expected) contribution
1	Little contribution - but attended group meetings
0	No contribution - did not attend group meetings*

    *   Where a rating of 4 or 0 is claimed please justify on the reverse of this form

3. Complete boxes A and C below in respect of your group and box B in respect of each individual group member and return this sheet to your tutor at the end of the tutorial.

    Box A

    Week: **Tutorial group**

    Box B

                                       Name

    Criteria

    1   ?
    2   ?
    3   ?
    4   ?

    TOTAL POINTS

Assessing using peer review

Box C

Name	**Name**
Presenter:	Handout prepared by:

Justification for award of 4:

Name:

Criterion / Criteria
marked 4:

Name:

Criterion / Criteria
marked 4:

Justification for award of 0:

Name:

Criterion / Criteria
marked 0:

Name:

Criterion / Criteria
marked 0:

Appendix B

Loughborough University Business School
Assessed introduction to banking tutorials

Peer review rating sheet

Instructions:

1.   Peer Review rating relates ONLY to your group's discussions before and during the tutorial.

2.   Insert a contribution rating for each criteria for each group member using the following key:

        4   Very significant contribution*
        3   Major contribution
        2   Satisfactory (expected) contribution
        1   Little contribution - but attended group meetings
        0   No contribution - did not attend group meetings*

    *   Where a rating of 4 or 0 is claimed please justify on the reverse of this form.

3.   Complete boxes A and C below in respect of your group and box B in respect of each individual group member and return this sheet to your tutor at the end of the tutorial.

    Box A

    Week: **Tutorial group:**

    Box B

                                     Name

    Criteria

    1.   Individual Participation
    2.   Team Spirit
    3.   Research / Preparation
    4.   Contributions to Tutorial

    TOTAL POINTS:

Assessing using peer review

Box C

Name	**Name**
Presenter	Handout prepared by:

NB: Tutor mark for content/presentation/discussion.......................... %

Justification for award of 4:

Name: Criterion / Criteria
                                                    marked 4:

Name: Criterion / Criteria
                                                    marked 4:

Justification for award of 0:

Name: Criterion / Criteria
                                                    marked 0:

Name: Criterion / Criteria
                                                    marked 0:

Appendix C

Peer Review Marks Sheet
Example

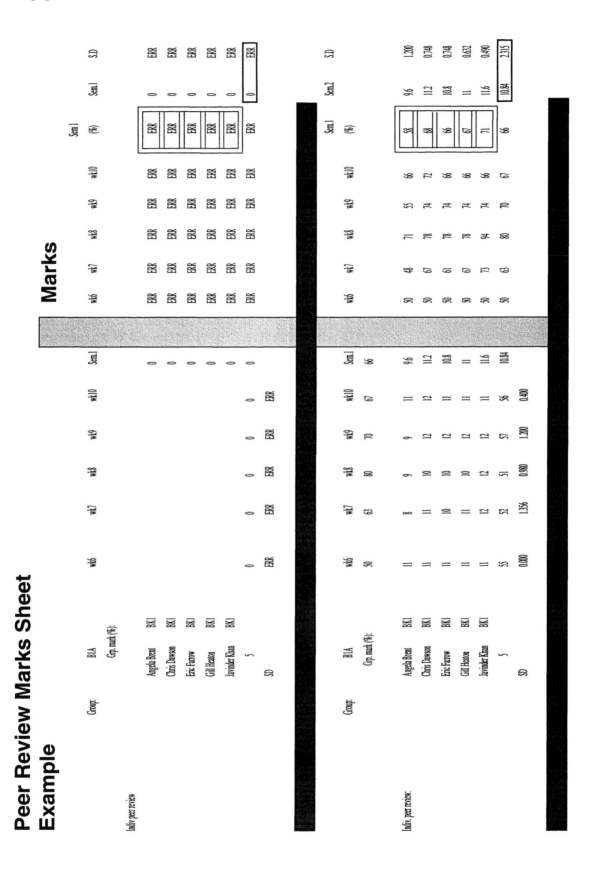

Marks

Appendix D

Extract of Coding and Formulae from Peer Review Marks Spreadsheet
(See Appendix C)

A:Al:	'PEER REVIEW MARKS SHEET
A:Fl:	'SEMESTER 1 1995/6
A:A2:	'Example:
A:L2:	'Individual marks
A:R3:	^Sem.1 av.
A:A4:	"Group:
A:B4:	^BIA
A:D4:	^wk6
A:E4:	^wk7
A:F4:	^wk8
A:G4:	^wk9
A:H4:	^wkl0
A:J4:	'Sem.1 av.
A:L4:	^wk6
A:M4:	^wk7
A:N4:	^wk8
A:04:	^wk9
A:P4:	^wklo
A:R4:	^(%)
A:T4:	'Sem.1 av.
A:U4:	^S.D
A:B5:	^Grp. mark
A:J 5:	@SUM(D5..H5)15
A:A6:	'Indiv. peer review:
A:B7:	'Angela Brent
A:C7:	'BKI
A:J7:	@SUM(D7..H7)15
A:L7:	(D5*BI2)*(D7/D12)
A:M7:	(E5*BI2)*(E7/E12)
A:N7:	(F5*BI2)*(F7/F12)
A:07:	(G5*B12)*(G7/G12)
A:P7:	(H5*BI2)*(H7/H12)
A:R7:	@SUM(L7..P7)/5
A:T7:	+J7
A:U7:	@STD(D7..H7)

Appendix E

Assessed introduction to banking tutorials
Rating sheet results - 1995-96 1st year BSc

Comments

- It was a very good module, and well organised.

- Good method of assessment. Good mix of long and short answer questions

- The module is very well organised, and it should not be changed in the future, as it is fine now.

- Peer Assessment encourages you to do more preparation so that you gain better marks.. Understanding of the topic is better through these tutorials.

- The opportunity to discuss the cases gives a better understanding of topics.

- Should have waited for results before filling this in!

- It has been a good way of learning the material, however it is fairly time consuming.

- It has helped to find out how others on my course rate my work and also it has shown me what 1 should be trying to achieve.

- I learnt a lot of banking knowledge from the "Peer Assessment". Also, I thought 1 improved "spoken English" through the presentation, didn't I?

- Very useful way of teaching, especially discussions and chance to work in teams.

- The work done in tutorials is very useful. And it's a great help towards the exams.

- Not really a good method of grading, as marks -can be fixed by groups. Different people have different attitudes, to the marking. So may fix grades.

- Maybe the grading could be carried out by individuals about their group.

- Keeps you awake. 9.00 too early for this kind of thing!!!

- It is useful for understanding the subject and will make it easier when having to remember information during tests etc.

- Too much work to do every week. Perhaps presentation every 2 weeks. Have to meet group 2 or 3 times a week which is quite alot and answer questions and prepare other people's questions.

- A definite experience. presentation technique. Useful for future careers.   Have definitely developed my

Assessing using peer review

- Lecturers are very handy in providing relevant information for material in tutorials. Experience to work in group - be peer assessed.

- The tutorials were a -good way of making us work in a team' and as a result cover a large range of material. Also the quick questions made us research material and as a result gain a lot of additional information not covered in lectures.

- The questions are a great way to get you into the library for some research - very helpful!

- Structurally very good, enhance learning commitment/effort.

- Very useful in bringing together the group.

- It is an interesting technique to assess students and enable them to study.

- It has been very helpful in revising for the end exam, plus reviewing the topics covered.

- Although it is necessary it seemed a lot of work for each tutorial for 5% of total marks. It is useful for revision of the course material and to cover more information ie, case law.

- Found it quite difficult to mark each other.

- 1 found this a very valuable way of studying. You get to make friends with members of your group whilst making sure that each week you keep up with the work set. Also gives a chance to get help from your peers if you need it.

- Difficult to decide on who gets the most points. All participated equally. Perhaps a confidential "point sheet" from each member so that a detailed opinion could be obtained.

- It helped getting to know classmates, helped with teamwork and made learning far more interesting than usual.

- Definitely worth pursuing this method of assessment in the future.

- Peer Assessment has enhanced my relationships with teams and other teams in the session.

- Good method of assessment.

- Particularly good at improving group work.

- Although Peer Assessment MAKES you work hard, in that fear of failure is a good motivator. I found that we did too much work, against the interests of other coursework.

- Most useful tutorial, with practical type experience.

- It was quite hard to define what fell into what criteria and hard to say aloud **esp** in opening weeks what the marks of colleagues were.

- Good means of motivation.

Peer assessment:

Report of a project involving group presentations and assessment by peers

Carole Mindham
Manchester Metropolitan University

"Self and peer assessment build on the awareness that most people have until it is knocked or mystified out of them" (Howard, 1991 p58).

Introduction

In recent years, Peer Assessment has come to be thought of by many people a 'fashionable' approach to the assessment of students. The advantages are described in terms of student involvement, active participation and the provision of worthwhile learning opportunities. Discussed to a lesser but equally extent valuable is the subject of the use of tutors' time. Tutors can become involved in the interaction which takes place during peer assessment, they may direct, or at least monitor, the learning processes rather than retiring to a quiet and isolated hermitage to read and mark essays and examination scripts. Brown and Dove put it quite bluntly,

> *"Active involvement by students in assessment can mean less boring assessment for the traditional assessor, the tutor and so assessment becomes a shared activity not a lonely one"* (Brown and Dove, 1991:60).

The traditional form of summative assessment, the examination, may be relevant for some courses where the learning of a body of knowledge and the ability to answer questions under exam conditions are required. It is possible, however, for a student to work for and be successful in both writing an essay and passing an examination without becoming a "deep" learner, without even fully comprehending the material.

This surface approach reduces what is to be learned to discrete facts, which can be learned by rote and regurgitated in exams. It includes memorising notes and often involves a lack of full understanding. Students following this approach are likely to deal with issues and areas of study in a superficial manner, unable to develop a logical argument. Such students will see learning as an increase in knowledge and information to be memorised.

> *"In a surface approach, what was to be learned was interpreted as the text itself In a deep approach the text was seen as the means through which to grapple with the meaning which underlay it"* (Marton, Hounsell and Entwistle, 1984 p197).

Peer assessment: Report of a project involving group presentations and assessment by peers

The premise of this discussion is that involving students in peer assessment and in a wider range of assessment tasks may encourage a 'deep' approach to learning. In addition, greater involvement in the assessment process may enhance its value as a learning opportunity.

In a deep approach, students will attempt to make sense of ideas and concepts by linking them to previous knowledge and understanding. These students will see learning as making sense and understanding reality. Marton and Saljo (1984) describe investigations into these approaches which show a close association between a deep approach to studying and success in university courses. It would appear that those who take a deep approach understand more, produce better written work, remember longer and gain higher marks than those who take a surface approach.

The CNAA Paper, Improving Student Learning (1992) highlights the key elements of courses which foster a deep approach.

- **Motivational interest.** Motivation is intrinsic with students experiencing a need to 'know'.

- **Active learning.** Students are actively involved rather than passive, developing independence.

- **Interaction with others.** Opportunities for discussion and exploratory talk.

- **A well structured knowledge base.** Content related to existing knowledge and taught in integrated wholes (CNAA, 1992).

Clearly, a deep approach is one which teachers at all levels would want to see students developing but with time constraints and rising numbers in Higher Education, opportunities to encourage this may be difficult to incorporate into overloaded programmes. One way forward may be to build it into the course itself, by utilising the assessment procedures.

"Whatever strategy is used students will be powerfully influenced by the assessment system they are working within" (CNAA, 1992).

Some assessment policies may actually encourage a shallow approach, these which including competition, memorising facts and written, timed examinations which do not ask for reflection or critical analysis.

"The very act of assessing is intrinsically 'learning by doing' - it involves the application of criteria, decision making, judgement and reflection. In other words, assessing is a 'deep' activity rather than a surface one and avoids the passivity which can pervade many less active forms of learning" (Race, 1993 p60).

In short, the learning experience involved in such a process is more important than the result of the assessment.

Peer assessment: Report of a project involving group presentations and assessment by peers

In Primary Schools teachers, aware of the necessity and indeed the legal requirement for assessment, attempt to build assessment tasks into their teaching in such a manner as to gather the information they need while providing learning activities. They are concerned that their pupils develop certain competences and they need to assess them so they attempt to make the assessment tasks part of the learning process. Perhaps we in Higher Education should learn from them. In Teacher Education courses it is quite feasible to devise tasks of relevance and value for intending teachers which will assess competences while providing learning opportunities. In addition, the students will see the very processes extolled as valuable, ie active learning, social interaction and appropriate assessment tasks, being incorporated into the teaching offered to them.

Involving students in the actual assessment procedures may be seen as an attempt to bring together several worthwhile objectives. We have already discussed here practical involvement in relevant tasks, assessment which provides learning opportunities and encouragement to adopt a 'deep' approach to learning. In addition several pieces of research suggest motivation is increased and results improved by involving students (Boyd and Cowan 1985, Falchikov, 1986, Boud, 1988)

> *"Ownership of the assessment process helps greatly in motivating students and encourages their active involvement in learning ... self and peer assessment motivate students to learn through assessment rather than regarding it as a separate and discrete process"* (Brown and Dove, 1991:60).

Self and peer assessment can demonstrate to participants the value of carefully structured and concise answers or presentations and the importance of close consideration of assessment criteria. Indeed Falchikov (1991) lists a wide range of benefits,

> *"Other benefits perceived by students to result from self and peer assessment include not only increases in learning, in critical ability, confidence and independence in individuals (Falchikov, 1986) in adaptability (Earl, 1986), but also in attitudes of responsibility towards other group members (Burnett and Cavay, 1980)"* (Falchikov in Brown and Dove, 1991p17).

With the advantages so clearly outlined in the literature, the present study was planned by tutors delivering a Professional Studies unit with Initial Teacher Education students. It must be said at this point that, while many of the advantages described were in fact noted during the project, there were also difficulties, some of them of a serious nature.

As this was the first year of a new BA in Primary Education Course, there was the opportunity to change existing structures. Students in the first year of this Course study all the subjects of the National Curriculum and they follow pedagogic studies in Education and Professional Studies (EPS). Consideration was given to building in as wide a range of assessment tasks as possible into this first year.

The tutors involved believe one important quality which student teachers must develop is the ability to work as part of a team, so it was felt that this should be incorporated into the task. As Jacques (1984) tells us, this skill must be learned and working within a small group could help this learning process. It was also a requirement that, unlike traditional forms of assessment which tend to test facts stored and existing knowledge, the students should gain knowledge and experience and develop skills from the assessment process itself Of course, peer assessment and group work may also, as Goldfinch and Raeside point out, "ease the marking burden on staff, allowing more staff time to be diverted to supervision and counselling and allowing quicker feedback to students" (1990 p210).

The assessment task

The planned project involved 160 students taught in eight groups, four preparing to teach children aged 3-7 (**Early Years Groups**), four preparing for the 7-11 age group (**Junior Groups**). Each of the eight groups were to work independently and were free to develop their own criteria for assessment.

In groups of three or four students would listen to a BBC Schools Radio programme or watch a Schools' TV programme. They were asked to critically evaluate it and to consider seven major points:-

- prior knowledge needed by the teacher

- prior knowledge needed by the child

- intended learning objectives

- possible follow-up work and differentiation

- resources needed

- areas for assessment

- the quality and value of teachers' notes provided.

Each small group would present their critical judgement to their Early Years or Junior Group who would assess the quality of the presentation and give a mark out of 50.

The objectives of this group task, presentation and assessment included:-

- to demonstrate the importance of the clear and concise presentation of views and information

- to add to students' understanding of the professional requirements of the teaching role

- to provide the opportunity for working responsibly with others and to anticipate problems and difficulties

- to gain some understanding of the value of schools broadcasts and the need to plan for and extend them.

Peer assessment: Report of a project involving group presentations and assessment by peers

Finally, each small group would allocate individual marks to members on the basis of their contribution to the group presentation. These would be out of 50 giving, with the group collaboration mark, a total of 100.

The last three weeks of the first Semester were devoted to the project, student contact time being three hours per week.

Peer assessment grid

Figure 1

Criteria	Groups				
	1	2	3	4	5

The process of the assessment tasks

Andresen, Nightingale, Boud and Magin (1993) describe a similar assessment model when an equal mark is given by staff to all members of a team based on the quality of the collaborative product. An equally weighted peer mark is added to this to reflect appraisal of each other's efforts and the average of the two awarded to each team member.

"This assessment model has been used successfully both for oral presentations and for written reports. In addition to modelling the collaborative environment in which students will eventually have to work professionally, the approach carries evident marking economies for staff" (Andresen et al, 1993 p53).

However, Gibbs, Habeshaw and Habeshaw (1986) (quoted in Conway et al) suggest that assessing group projects in this way may present problems with and between groups and we would endorse that warning. As Burnett and Cavay (1980) found, our students, while entering into the project willingly, found the responsibility for making peer assessments a most uncomfortable experience.

Week One

The students, in eight groups of approximately 20, were reminded of the overall objectives of the project. The task was clearly outlined ie, the presentation of a critical evaluation of a schools' broadcast, either radio or television and of the accompanying teachers' notes. The process of assessing the final presentations was considered and the need for assessment criteria discussed.

"Whatever the purpose of a particular piece of assessment, students need to know the criteria by which their effort will be judged. Communicating these criteria is an essential prior stage to the assessment act itself"(Andresen, Nightingale, Boud and Magin, 1993 p13).

The knowledge of criteria is clearly a prerequisite before beginning the task and certainly before assessing. Many students facing peer assessment for the first time will feel uncomfortable, inadequate or inexperienced.

"The key to solving problems of this nature is clarification of assessment criteria. When criteria are phrased in language that learners can readily understand, their reservations about being able to make judgements based on the criteria are rapidly dispelled" (Race, 1993:58).

The students were asked to determine the criteria by which their Early Years or Junior group would judge the final presentations. Phil Race outlines quite clearly the advantages of students providing assessment criteria for themselves.

"Where it is possible to draw assessment criteria from learners themselves, especially in group situations, the sense of ownership which learners develop is very powerful and leads to them using the criteria with considerable enthusiasm" (1993 p51).

The Peer Assessment Grid devised by Phil Race (1993) was adapted to carry five criteria (10 marks for each) and spaces for marking up to six presentations. Figure 1.

Peer assessment: Report of a project involving group presentations and assessment by peers

After discussion a set of criteria was identified by each of the eight groups, the main emphases were similar although some groups decided on differential marks as they felt some criteria were worth more than others.

Examples of Group Criteria: Figure 2

Junior Group	**Marks**
1. Does the presentation address the evaluative points given as important?	10
2. Consideration for interest and variety	10
3. Does it have clarity and coherence?	10
4. Relevant use of resources	10
5. Is there equal participation	10

Early Years Group	**Marks**
1. Interest level	10
2. Content (the seven points given)	10
3. Quality (analysis, criticism, evaluation)	10
4. Visual aids and resources	10
5. Structure (teamwork, flow)	10

Junior Group	**Marks**
1. Relevance to evaluative points	15
2. Critical analysis of evaluative points	20
3. Clarity and interest of delivery	10
4. Use of resources	5

Peer assessment: Report of a project involving group presentations and assessment by peers

Early Years Group	Marks
1. Critical evaluation	10
2. Research (the seven given points plus others)	15
3. Presentation (clear structure, smooth, easily understood, right level, body language, clarity of voice)	15
4. Visual aids	10

It was decided by the students that each Early Years or Junior group, when assessing presentations, would watch all of those within their group before making final decisions on marks.

Armed with the assessment criteria for their group, the students, in friendship groups of two, three or four, were given a pack containing a schools' programme (Radio or Television) and the teachers' notes to study. They then began the Assessment Task.

Week Two
The second session began with each group reviewing the criteria determined the previous week with the option of making changes if required.

This was followed by a discussion on the process to be adopted for allocating individual marks. We followed a similar system to that outlined by Andresen et al (1993) and Falchikov (1988) with the group mark (out of 50) given by members of other, similar groups, and individual marks (out of 50) given by fellow group members.

Conway, Kember, Sivan and Wu describe a system of peer assessment undertaken by their students on an optometry course at Hong Kong Polytechnic.

> "The first time the project method was used, the students found the group projects interesting and more effective than lectures for most aspects of learning. The only significantly negative elements of student feedback concerned the fairness of assessment" (1993 p45).

Clearly, within a group it may be that not all members contribute equally, resulting in an unfair workload for some and an easy time for others.

Each of the eight Early Years and Junior groups of students involved in this project discussed in depth the fairest way for a small group to allocate individual marks. Some groups felt they needed criteria by which to judge an individual's contribution while others felt, in such small groups, they were unnecessary and marks could be fairly allocated by open discussion. The tutor, while monitoring each group's discussion was not a part of it but, with each group, she introduced an adaptation of Brown and Dove's list of Task and Maintenance functions (1991 p26), not to use for rating peers as Brown and Dove did in their research but to raise awareness of the attributes, skills and qualities different individuals can bring to a group project (see Figure 3).

Figure 3

Group projects: contributions

1. Information and Opinion Giver - offers facts, opinions suggestions etc.
2. Asks for facts, opinions, ideas to help group discussion.
3. Starter: proposes goals and tasks to initiate action.
4. Direction giver: develops plans, focuses on the task.
5. Co-ordinator: pulls together ideas, summarises.
6. Diagnoser: figures out problems in the group.
7. Feasibility tester: examines ideas for workability.
8. Evaluator: compares ideas, raises standards.
9. Encourager: encourages everyone to participate.
10. Harmoniser and Compromiser.
11. Tension Reliever, eases tension, increases enjoyment.
12. Communication Helper.
13. Active Listener, receptive to others' ideas.
14. Trust Builder, encourages individuality.
15. Link Person, builds liaison.
16. Time Keeper.
17. Other?

(Adapted from Brown and Dove, 1991 p26).

Criteria for individual marks

Examples of criteria identified for use by small groups to help in allocating individual marks for personal contribution. All of the friendship groups in one Early Years Group used these:-

Figure 4

1.	Amount of work, research, resources	15
2.	Attitude (motivation, encouragement, organisation, keeping group on task)	15
3.	Evaluation, opinions, criticism	10
4.	Practical teaching aspects	10

One friendship group (Early Years) identified just two criteria:-

1.	Effort (work done, how well researched)	25
2.	Attitude (motivation, organisation, encouragement etc)	25

Peer assessment: Report of a project involving group presentations and assessment by peers

Week Three

The small friendship groups presented their critiques to their peers within their groups of around 20. These presentations varied widely in quality, all groups fulfilled the requirements and addressed the seven points listed but some made good use of resources, artifacts and visual aids while other groups had none. The quality of critical debate varied as did the quality of actual presentation. Some individuals 'performed' while others merely read from a script. One group presented their findings and opinions in the form of a debate which appeared to be spontaneous and 'live' but, in reality, must have been most carefully prepared. Another group played the video of their programme, without sound, throughout their presentation and timed their comments to fit the excerpts on screen.

Students used the Peer Assessment Grid (Figure I.) on which to enter their criteria and record marks. They marked independently in the first instance then small groups collaborated to present a group assessment for each presentation.

The first group had no qualms about marking the presentations and were happy to give marks publicly. The following, and subsequent groups, however, wanted their marks to be given anonymously. Marks were collected, written on the board and then averaged, final marks were rounded up or down where necessary. Each member of the group received the same final mark for the presentation. Following this allocation of group marks for collaborative work, each small group considered individual contributions in order to distribute individual marks.

Problems which arose in week three

Absentees. Clearly, if a student missed the presentation s/he could not 're-sit'. Each case was dealt with separately.

(i) One student was absent through illness on the day but friends in her group felt she had contributed a fair share to the discussions and preparation and, having only missed the actual presentation, they decided she should receive the group mark along with themselves.

(ii) One student missed some of the preparation but played a large part in the presentation. His group decided he deserved the same group mark but a lower individual mark.

(iii) One group was angry when a member failed to appear for the presentation, they felt he was not taking the assessment seriously. The two remaining students went so far as to search for him. However, he appeared later having had an injury and been to the hospital. It was decided that he could, having eventually taken part in the presentation, have the same group mark as his fellow group members but he must earn his personal mark by submitting his critique for the tutor to mark.

(iv) Three students missed too much of the project to qualify for assessment and so submitted written critiques of the programmes.

Peer assessment: Report of a project involving group presentations and assessment by peers

- The students were critical of some aspects of the marking system. They were warned that highly inflated marks would be unacceptable, over 80% (ie in the first class honours bracket) could only be awarded for exceptional work. It was indicated that, to avoid this situation, they should be wary of giving over 40 in either marking category. Some students believed this was unfair and felt strongly that 40/50 was not sufficient for a well presented piece of work. As one student wrote in her Final Comment, "Putting an upper limit on the scoring system was patronising and irrelevant."

- As the presentations progressed tutors became very aware of the lack of moderation. Marking was, on the whole, fair and ranking reasonable but, as there was no moderation across groups, some excellent presentations received only the same marks as mediocre ones from another group.

Each of the eight groups found the marking of small group presentations was not too difficult. The criteria were vital, they helped students to be clear in their judgements and ensured that all the identified, important areas were recognised. The last group to attend this session, however, was a disaster and pointed to the problem of group relationships identified by other researchers in this field (Conway et al, 1993, Gibbs et al, 1986).

Personality clashes interfered with the group marking procedures but, unfortunately this was not obvious until after the session when marks had been allocated. Two very low marks were given (17 and 19), this should have been queried as no presentation was of such poor quality as to warrant these marks (at Fail level). All of the groups found the allocating of individual marks extremely difficult and stressful. The majority decided on equal marks as they felt all had contributed equally, but even those groups found it difficult to set a level on their efforts. Those groups which gave differential marks appeared to discuss the matter carefully and to allocate marks within an agreed framework. The differential aspect was less of a problem than the initial decision on personal worth and where to set the median.

Both of these solutions involved comprehensive discussion and peer assessment and those taking part were aware of the benefits of the process. However, there were several groups who dispensed with any pretence at fair marking or consideration for criteria, the students simply decided upon a reasonable final grade, usually around 60, and added the requisite figure to that already gained for the collaborative presentation. The result was, not exactly arbitrary, but an 'equalised' mark given without due thought to value of contribution and consequently it was almost worthless.

Student comments

1. At the beginning of the Course Unit, the assessment task was outlined to the students and they were asked a) if they had been involved in Peer Assessment before and b) to write down their immediate reactions to the information. From 163 responses 19 had taken part in Peer Assessment previously. Of these, 11 gave positive responses while 7 were less impressed and all of this last group expressed concern about personalities within any group affecting assessment procedures. Some of the initial reactions included the following statements:-

Peer assessment: Report of a project involving group presentations and assessment by peers

1.	It sounds like a good idea	48
2.	It sounds like a bad idea	3
3.	It could be a fair assessment	19
4.	It could be an unfair assessment	61
5.	Students expressing 'apprehension' and 'trepidation' (their words)	53
6.	It sounds interesting and worthwhile	12
7.	This could damage or split the group	3
8.	This could help group co-operation	5
9.	This should give us confidence	2
10.	This could damage confidence	5
11.	This gives us responsibility and control of our learning	4
12.	This should be fun	4
13.	This will be hard	4
14.	This will be better than an exam	12

These reactions may be roughly grouped into, Positive, 106 and Concerned, 129.

Those responses which do not fit into the categories above included

"A brilliant idea because it will get everyone much more involved"
"Wonderful"
"What a great way of assessing work"
"You get out what you put in"
"A little shocked and worried"
"Will we mark each other too highly for fear of offending friends?"
"I would prefer to be assessed by an unbiased tutor"
"Frightening"
"The idea sounds original but the danger is that people's opinions of another person may be assessed rather than the work that person did"
"Oh no, 1 hope the rest of the group like me otherwise 1 may be marked down"
"Panic"
"I'm not looking forward to that, it sounds dreadful"
"Sheer horror"
"Nightmare"
"I don't want to do it, very nervous"
"Help!"
"Initial response dread - although it's a good idea for professional development."

2. The Likert scale (Figure 5) completed in Week 2 of the project by 147 students, involved the questions:-

   1. Students should play a part in assessment
   2. The final grade will be a fair reflection
   3. This is a fair way to divide marks
   4. Peers can assess fairly
   5. This is an appropriate assessment method
   6. The assessment has been clearly explained.

Figure 5.   Likert Scale (after Conway, Kember, Sivan and Wu, 1993).

We hope you have enjoyed taking part in this process and would welcome your opinion.

Please place a tick on the scales to indicate your response.

1	2	3	4	5

Strongly
disagree

Strongly
agree

1.   Students should play a part in assessment.

1	2	3	4	5

2.   The final grade will be a fair reflection.

1	2	3	4	5

3.   This is a fair way to divide marks (Group 50% Individual 50%).

1	2	3	4	5

4.   Peers can assess fairly.

1	2	3	4	5

5.   This is an appropriate assessment method.

1	2	3	4	5

6.   The assessment has been clearly explained.

1	2	3	4	5

Figure 6. Graph to show the results of the Likert Scale Questionnaire.

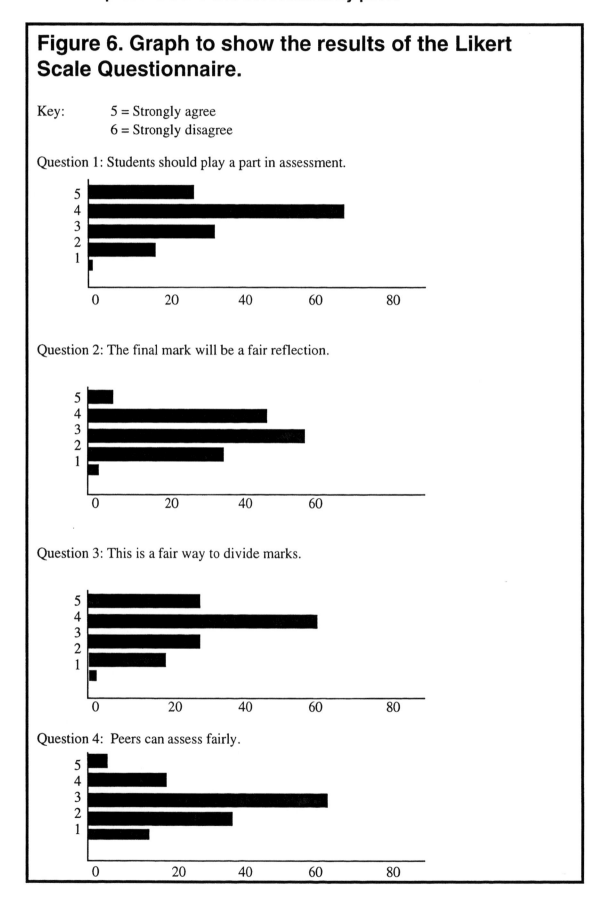

Key: 5 = Strongly agree
         6 = Strongly disagree

Question 1: Students should play a part in assessment.

Question 2: The final mark will be a fair reflection.

Question 3: This is a fair way to divide marks.

Question 4: Peers can assess fairly.

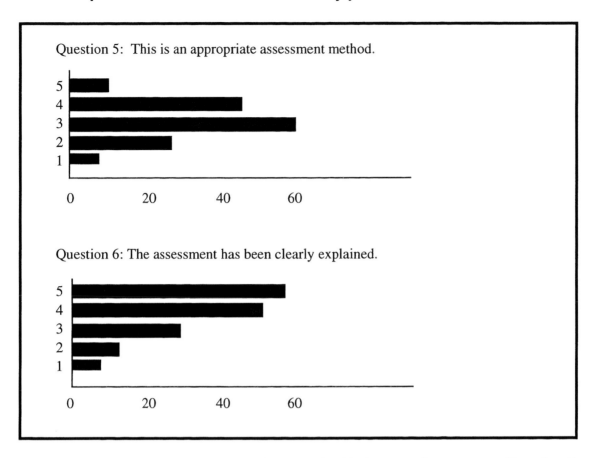

Question 5: This is an appropriate assessment method.

Question 6: The assessment has been clearly explained.

It would seem that students on the whole felt they should play a part in assessment (Question 1) and that the project was an appropriate assessment method (Question 5). They believed the combination of two marks was acceptable (Question 3) and, while they thought the final mark ought to be a fair reflection of standard (Question 2) they were less sure that peers would actually assess fairly (Question 4).

On completion of the assessment

The responses collected on completion of the project and the assessment revealed an extraordinarily wide range of opinions. Sadly, many students who responded positively before the exercise found it so difficult and stressful that they changed their views. It is also obvious that groups had varying experiences depending, it would appear, on relationships within the group. The group described as a disaster were obviously unhappy with group assessment but, on reading the Final Comments it became clear that at least two other groups had experienced the same problem. Many subscribed to the view that "It is difficult to judge friends along with those less well liked" (student) while the word "bitchiness" appeared in five comments and one student explained "if they mark us down then we will mark them down." Another student's Final Comment includes this point "I think the exercise has been successful as far as it goes, though 1 still find that my preconceived ideas of the individuals involved tended to influence the mark, no matter how impartial I tried to be." The relationships within a group are obviously going to play a large part in determining the success or otherwise of this form of assessment. The distribution of individual marks which proved very difficult for many students was expressed clearly, "We both felt it inappropriate to give each other too low a mark, yet are too modest to give ourselves near full marks."

Peer assessment: Report of a project involving group presentations and assessment by peers

It also emerged that some small groups had not complied with the timing which allowed ten minutes for each presentation. In consequence there were groups which ran over time by as much as 20 minutes which was seen as a) unfair and b) made the session too long.

One student comment was worrying, "I feel that this kind of assessment will increase competition, it could become very competitive." As this is one of the areas peer assessment aims to overcome, this will need careful consideration if the project is repeated.

A very valid point was raised regarding feedback. It transpired that some groups where presentations ran to time, had sufficient time left to discuss the session and for groups and tutor to offer advice on improvement. Those groups found this valuable. Those groups who ran over the allotted three hours did not have time for this and some students commented on the lack of feedback.

As with the original reactions, many of the final comments can be categorised: although not quantified in the usual way.

1.	It is a good idea	22
2.	It is a bad idea	4
3.	It was a fair assessment	1.0
4.	It was an unfair assessment	25
5.	It was harrowing/worrying	8
6.	It was worthwhile	1.6
7.	This was a good experience	1.6
8.	This was very difficult	33
9.	The tutor should have some in-put	20.

Some of the positive comments included:-

"I now think it is a good idea. I was skeptical at first but having passed through the motions I realise it is quite a fair way to assess a group. Providing personality clashes do not play a part then it should be continued."

"Peer assessment, I feel, is an extremely fair way of marking work. It takes the pressure off the presenters and may allow a higher quality of work to emerge. With the elimination of a single assessor and consequently a single mark, the average mark given by numerous peers should be a fairer reflection."

Clearly there has been a very mixed reaction to the project but it would also seem that some groups experienced more tension and stress than others.

Tentative conclusions

Although both students and staff found the marking system stressful they all agreed that a) the project itself was worthwhile and should be repeated and b) Peer Assessment could be a valuable learning experience, indeed many students felt they had gained insight, skills and understanding from this experience.

1. Objectives

If we refer back to the objectives of the project we find that they were all achieved to varying degrees.

- The students participated in group discussion in several contexts, all of them demanding a high degree of participation and, when assessing, a responsible and professional attitude was demonstrated by all groups.

- During these discussions and in the presentations there were opportunities for comparison of views, opinions and critical analysis.

- The importance of the clear and concise presentation of views and information was clearly demonstrated.

- The students' understanding of the professional requirements of the teaching role was increased.

- There was ample opportunity for working responsibly with others and for anticipating problems and difficulties.

- All the students involved gained some understanding of the value of schools' broadcasts and the need to plan for and extend them. In addition they were introduced to a wide range of radio and TV programmes for schools.

2. Assessment as part of the Learning Process

This Education and Professional Studies unit deals with pedagogical aspects of the Primary teacher's role including the examination of group work, assessment, collaborative learning and active learning. All of these issues, and more, demand reflection, debate and some personal experience. Many of them could be incorporated; not only into the critical examination of the programmes but also into the discussion and professionalism involved in using criteria and assessing peers.

Self evaluation is a skill we encourage amongst our students. Their Personal Development Profile is becoming a most important part of their Course and will go with them as they begin their teaching career. Peer evaluation, the discussion, negotiation and sharing of views, it was felt, would contribute towards self evaluative skills and the reflective attitude we hope they will develop.

Peer assessment: Report of a project involving group presentations and assessment by peers

If the project is repeated several areas will need to be adjusted.

3. Standardisation

Not all groups followed the same routine. For consistency and to contribute to the moderation process it would be beneficial to have all procedures carefully listed and planned so that tutors leading the sessions were providing the same, or at least similar experiences for all students. For example;

(i) The advice to make notes and consider marks throughout each presentation, marks to be readjusted at the end, rather than merely viewing throughout, should be given to all students.

(ii) Point out to all students that not everyone in the small group needs to 'perform' in the presentation, people have different strengths to offer to the group (Brown and Dove's list of Task and Maintenance Functions).

(iii) More time should be spent on discussing the criteria for assessing group work. The students appreciated the opportunity to compile their own list but not all of them were clear about allocating marks ie, if 10 points were available for visual aids and resources, what constituted 4 and what constituted 7? The process of discussion to make this type of decision is part of the learning process and the students need help to appreciate it as such.

(iv) If the system of marking described here, where group marks were entered on a chart, totalled then averaged, is repeated, then it needs to be standardised. Some groups entered their marks as they were decided upon which could have influenced those groups still involved in discussion. A fairer procedure would be to hold all marks and enter them on the chart only when all were finalised.

4. Moderation

This must be the major concern if we attempt to include peer assessment in future courses. The project described was a new venture for staff and for most of the students and, even after reading of the experiences of others, we were still extremely naive and unprepared for the effects of personalities and relationships. As Balla and Boyle (1994) point out, traditional assessment is losing its relevance.

"It is becoming more widely accepted that no one method of student assessment best suits all instructional objectives and evaluative purposes. Good practice in assessment of student performance is associated with selection of the method which matches the purposes of the assessment, the properties or characteristics being assessed and the objectives of instruction" (Balla and Boyle, 1994 p19).

Peer assessment: Report of a project involving group presentations and assessment by peers

Above all it must be fair. Most systems of assessment contain flaws, so peer assessment can be expected to have its share. If it is to be sustained as a system of assessment then moderation must take priority as an area for attention. In this instance some presentations of a very high standard gained average marks from peers while lesser presentations in another group received inflated marks. Two major issues were identified here.

    (i)   Inter-personal relationships, inflated marks given to friends or vice versa and

    (ii) No comparisons across groups were possible.

A system whereby the large groups could view a range of presentations across the year group before deciding marks could help. The use of video and extending the time available to two three hour sessions rather than one could be considered.

Clearly a major problem surfaced when members of the large group allowed personal friendships and animosity to influence their marking of small group presentations. This did not apply to all groups and is perhaps a reminder that group dynamics can play a very large part in the responses displayed by students. As the large groups tend to be compact and independent of each other, one solution could be for a group to mark the presentations of another group. In that way personal relationships would not enter into the decisions. This was by far the major criticism and accords with the comments made by students in Conway, Kember, Sivan and Wu's (1993) research. In the original comments and in the responses to the Likert Scale this was an area listed by many students as one of concern and clearly, their concerns were justified.

If the project is repeated, the organisation of group marking must avoid the possibility of personality clashes, poor relationships and peer pressure influencing judgements and negating the benefits of peer assessment.

Many students felt the most difficult task was the designation of individual marks for effort and contribution to the group project. While the assessment task itself was felt to be useful and worthwhile, both staff and students found the marking procedure cumbersome, difficult and, in some cases, unfair. A less complicated method would be for the large group to award a mark out of 100 for each small group presentation. This would be followed by discussion within each small group to determine if each member deserved equal rating. Before the project, all students agreed that it was often felt to be unfair when, in a group, one person was left to do all the work while another did none. In the final event, this variable in-put frequently is not evident. In this project most groups decided on equal marks for group members (30 small groups out of a total of 41) but the negotiation which took place where equal marks were felt to be inappropriate was conscientiously and amicably entered into and decisions reached were accepted without ill feeling.

In conclusion, the task itself, the team work involved, the discussion, the shared experiences, the joint responsibility and the final presentations were all judged by staff and students to be worthwhile and valid for assessment purposes. The major problems lay in the assessment procedures. Most of the objectives of the project were successfully covered and it was certainly seen as of more value than an examination or an essay. However, the lack of moderation procedures, the effect of personal relationships and the 'equalising' of marks by some students were found to be unforeseen and unacceptable elements of the project. If it is to be repeated then all of the points listed will need to be addressed and adjustments made in order to arrive at a fair result and to realise the full potential of peer assessment.

References

Andresen, L, Nightingale, P, Boud, D and Magin, D (1993) *Strategies for Assessing Students* SCED (Standing Conference on Educational Development, Birmingham) Paper 78.

Balla, J and Boyle, P (1994) Evaluation of Student Performance: a framework for improving practice *Assessment and Evaluation in Higher Education* 19 (1) pp. 17-28.

Boud, D (1988) *Developing Student Autonomy in Learning* Kogan Page, London.

Boyd, H and **Cowan, J** (1986) *A case for self assessment* Assessment and Evaluation in Higher Education 10, 3, 225-35.

Brown, S and Dove, P (1991) *Self & Peer Assessment* SCED, Paper 63.

Burnett, W and Cavay, G (1980) Peer Assessment by Fifth Year Students of Surgery *Assessment in Higher Education* 5 (3) pp.273-278.

Conway, R, Kember, D, Sivan, A and Wu, M (1993) Peer Assessment of an Individual's Contribution to a Group Project *Assessment & Evaluation in Higher Education* 1993, Vol 18 No 1 pp.45-46.

CNAA (1992) *Improving Student Learning* Oxford Centre for Staff Development, Oxford Polytechnic.

Earl, SE (1986) Staff and Peer Assessment - measuring an individual's contribution to group performance *Assessment and Evaluation in Higher Education* 11 (1) pp.60-69.

Falchikov, N (1986) Self and peer assessment of a group project designed to promote the skills of capability *Programmed Learning and Educational Technology* 25 (4) pp.327-339.

Falchikov, N (1988) Product comparisons and process benefits of collaborative peer group and self assessment *Assessment & Evaluation in Higher Education* 11 (2) pp. 146-165.

Falchikov, N (1991) in Brown, S and Dove, P (1991).

Gibbs, G, Habeshaw, S and Habeshaw, T (1986) *53 Interesting ways to Assess Your Students* Bristol Technical and Educational Services.

Peer assessment: Report of a project involving group presentations and assessment by peers

Goldfinch, J and Raeside, R (1990) Development of a Peer Assessment Technique for obtaining Individual Marks on a Group Project *Assessment & Evaluation in Higher Education* Vol 15 No 3 pp.210-23 1.

Howard, Joanna (1991) Self and Peer Assessment in Brown, S and Dove, P 1991 *SCED Paper 63*.

Jacques, D (1984) *Learning in Groups* Groom Helm, London.

Marton, F, Hounsell, D and Entwistle, N (1984) *The Experience of Learning* Scottish Academic Press.

Marton, F and Saljo (1984) in Marton, F, Hounsell, D and Entwistle, N Scottish Academic Press.

Race, P (1993) *Never Mind The Teaching - Feel the Learning* SEDA (Staff and Educational Development Association, Birmingham) Paper 80.

Lessons from coming of age in peer assessment and group work

Hazel Fullerton & Yacub Rafiq
University of Plymouth

Days of yore

For centuries lecturers, students and external examiners shared assumptions about assessment, how it would be conducted, how it was, had been and presumably it always would be. Unchallenged, it reinforced the status quo comfortably until the 80s.

In tracking the route taken by our own institution, this article reveals efforts to make the challenge and draws in similar experiences across the HE sector over the late 80s and early 90s. It takes into account disenchantment with existing approaches and the need to find ways of coping with changes in terms of numbers and the very purposes of higher education itself. The great value of the process has been that the design of assessments is now given very serious thought and in the effort to ensure that time is spent effectively and assessment has become a much more integral part of the learning.

Conception

There were rumblings, a growing intolerance about the amount of regurgitation that was appearing from the exam suites. Disquiet about the limitations of traditional assessment approaches had been growing for ideological reasons and there was questioning about whether the assessment was actually contributing to the learning process.

Knowing how much lecturers themselves learn through marking, there was a convincing argument that that involvement in the process of assessment could make a valuable contribution to learning, so peer assessment of essay assignments was introduced to a course for new lecturers in the FE/HE sector. Shock. Horror. At first, the group needed reassurance that a course tutor would mark it too and some negotiated to have more than one peer to comment. The distinction between marking (summative assessment) and commenting (formative assessment) suddenly became clear to them. Thus peer marking pairs and triads were formed. Success. Enthusiasm. They leapt into the feedback discussion with vigour - over coffee - over lunch - in the pub - the debates ranged and raged. This was learning! Soon 'marks' became less important, pass/fail was OK, what mattered was the feedback and discussion.

At the same time there was growing concern (perhaps highlighted by the rigours of CNAA procedures) that learning objectives should be more explicit. That was followed the influence of the Enterprise in Higher Education (EHE) initiative which focused strongly on developing students' transferable skills to enable them to contribute more holistically to the world of employment. This spotlight on skills and how to gauge if they are being achieved further highlighted the shortcomings of the assessment system. The debate now centred on what was being learnt and how that could be established.

So these triggers for change in assessment were already in place when the sudden huge increase in student numbers hit the UK. Now in the era of large groups, the lecturers were finding that although lecturing to 300 instead of 40 was a shock, it was manageable whereas marking six sets of 300 essays was not. Previous concerns about reliability of assessment moved from disquiet to desperation. The system could not cope, a new one had to be conceived and created.

Infancy

One of the group involved in thinking about the learning power of peer assessment as described above, took the process back into his engineering faculty and introduced it into problem-solving tutorials (Fry 1990). The reason was his frustration that only a few of his students were carrying out the problems in advance of the tutorial and waited passively for him to perform them for the class, serving them solutions on a plate. The system he introduced involved students simply swapping papers with the person sitting next them. They would tackle each problem in turn, and one student who felt reasonably confident about a problem would work it through on the board. The tutor would then go over it, allocating marks to the various parts and explaining his rationale and discussing and taking questions about alternative approaches to the solution. Using this model the students would mark their neighbour's solution. Occasionally students would seek reassurance on a point but generally they were fairly confident.

The added value was that they started to understand the rules of the game; how marking worked; that there were a range of ways of tackling any one problem; understanding the need for 'workings' to be shown to communicate thinking and an developing a better sense of proportion of how to approach questions. The lecturer was prepared to arbitrate in disputes, but they were rare. By now the students were doing the work in advance lest they let themselves down in front of their peers and it was only a few weeks before the group asked that the marks be taken into account in their final summative score.

Lesson one - allow the students a chance to see that peers can mark reliably.

Early lessons

The next lessons came from EHE which introduced many valuable approaches. One of these was where whole modules were introduced in which the content of the discipline was used, but in such a way as to enable the development and record the achievement of transferable skills. Self assessment and peer assessment were now introduced, both to handle the process and to increase

Lessons from coming of age in peer assessment and group work

the students' awareness and judgement of these, often subjective areas. 'Skills mapping' sheets were developed to help identify the skills and note if they had been demonstrated. This was not universally accepted by the students or many of the staff who were still encumbered with the expectations or traditional methods and did not necessarily agree that higher education should have any responsibility for the wider range of student skills. Where these problems were overcome, the process worked relatively well and were accepted as a part of the degree.

Lesson two - ensure all parties have the opportunity to grasp the rationale for the change and are able to see the benefits to their education.

Selling the rationale was harder than it may sound. At that time students retained very traditional expectations of what assessment 'ought' to be and hadn't noticed the accompanying warts. Many thought the new techniques meant that they were being short changed by lecturers who were trying to get away with doing less work. This was especially true for second and third year students who had experienced the more traditional assessment fare. In the future, as students pay for increasing proportions of their higher education, it is likely that these attitudes will resurface.

Lesson three -if you are going to introduce something new, introduce it initially with first years before expectations are too entrenched.

This era overlapped with the increase of student numbers. In casting around for survival strategies, the institution organised a series of 'change agents' programmes each of which addressed a particular focus. Two or three representatives from each faculty were given relevant literature and came together for training and awareness raising in a variety of techniques within a particular topic. It was then their job, as change agents, to return to their faculties and spread the good word.

The Assessment programme was particularly successful with the underlying values eg reliability, relevance, avoiding bias, and making criteria explicit coming clearly onto the common agenda. The techniques which proved to be of greatest interest were objective testing, group work, use of portfolios, attachment sheets and peer assessment. The latter two were used together in tackling some of the problems with student seminar presentations. Previously students had not been bothering to listen to others or were only turning up to those tutorials during which they themselves would be presenting. This had been doubly frustrating, as the process was intended to actually deliver parts of the syllabus. By involving the students in identifying and weighting appropriate criteria, staff were agreeably surprised at how sensibly students did this and that they arrived at the same kind of decisions and distribution that they themselves would have done. Using these to design attachment sheets and to allocate marks to the rest of their cohort, the students learnt to understand the criteria, make judgments and in turn reflect on and apply their observations to improving their own performance. Variations were negotiated, for example some groups were happy to mark the presentation skills but wanted the tutor to award a mark for the content. This sharing out of responsibilities crops up in a few of the schemes and seems to reassure most of the parties most of the time.

Lesson four - involve the students in the process wherever possible.

Adolescence and learning from mistakes

Not all early experimentation was successful. In areas of the institution, some had been embraced with such an unexpected degree of enthusiasm that 'born-again' tutors introduced group and peer assessment to their classes without realising that their colleagues were doing likewise and students were having the same experiences in many modules. Although it would be an exaggeration to say that some students were never being assessed in their own right or by a tutor, this duplication clearly was not appropriate and external examiners tended to look askance.

Lesson four - avoid inadvertently replacing one monoculture (eg all essays) with another - by co-ordinating assessment strategies along and across pathways and programmes.

It worked the other way as well of course. Students who met some of the new techniques in some modules were becoming more aware of their own learning process and the benefits of alternative approaches. They would then complain to their other lecturers that, "The way that Dr.X does this works much better and could you please get your act together?"

Lesson five - there is a critical mass beyond which alternative techniques can invade the whole system.

Peer assessment of group work

It was now being used regularly for group work. This coped well with large numbers as, although the tutor probably spent longer marking a group project than an individual one, the number of projects was cut by at least a quarter. The group work also developed the EHE-fostered skills such as team work, collaboration, time and task management. However, using the approach of the tutor awarding a group mark for a piece of work and giving the group responsibility for dividing that mark proportionally amongst the group members didn't always work well. Sometimes groups simply agreed to share marks equally and in other cases it caused social upheaval - 'I had been friends with Y for two and a half years before this, and I'm never going to speak to him again!' Although the tutor concerned was available to arbitrate in disputes, damage was done.

Lesson seven ... gather responses from individuals in confidence, in exam conditions or handed in to the departmental office.

The process was formalised further to promote fairness and to make students more aware of the skills they were acquiring. The students had four marks to distribute to the other members - against each of the particular skills and/or the contributions to the major tasks of the project as shown in the figure below (they did not allocate themselves any marks).

Lessons from coming of age in peer assessment and group work

Distribution of marks across the team

	TASKS					SKILLS				TOTAL
	survey	draft plan	final plan	costing		ideas	team work	leader-ship	negot-iation	
Tom					Tom					
Dick	1	2	1	1	Dick	1	1	2	1	**10**
Harry	1	1	1	2	Harry	1	2	0	1	**9**
Harriet	2	1	2	1	Harriet	2	1	2	2	**13**

score attributed by Tom

	TASKS					SKILLS				TOTAL
	survey	draft plan	final plan	costing		ideas	team work	leader-ship	negot-iation	
Tom	2	2	2	1	Tom	1	1	1	1	**11**
Dick					Dick					
Harry	1	1	1	2	Harry	1	1	1	1	**9**
Harriet	1	1	1	1	Harriet	2	2	2	2	**12**

marks attributed by Dick

	TASKS					SKILLS				TOTAL
	survey	draft plan	final plan	costing		ideas	team work	leader-ship	negot-iation	
Tom	2	2	1	1	Tom	1	1	1	1	**10**
Dick	1	1	1	1	Dick	2	2	0	1	**9**
Harry					Harry					
Harriet	1	1	2	2	Harriet	1	1	3	2	**13**

marks attributed by Harry

	TASKS					SKILLS				TOTAL
	survey	draft plan	final plan	costing		ideas	team work	leader-ship	negot-iation	
Tom	2	1	2	1	Tom	1	1	2	1	**11**
Dick	1	1	1	1	Dick	2	2	1	2	**11**
Harry	1	2	1	2	Harry	1	1	1	1	**10**
Harriet					Harriet					

marks attributed by Harriet

Figure 1

The marks for each individual from every group member, can then be totalled; Tom has 32 / Dick 30 / Harry 28 / Harriet 38. The appropriate proportion of the project mark can then be allocated (by office staff or post grad. assistants?) to each student.

As the overall project was awarded 80% - Tom gets 80%, Dick 75%, Harry 70% and Harriet 95%.

This is arrived at by calculating a group average (project mark divided by the number of students in the group multiplied by the number of tasks/skills) in this case $\frac{80}{(4 \times 8)}$ giving an average of 2.5

Then that average is multiplied by the individual's score (eg in Dick's case 2.5 x 30 = 75%)

Thus the approach started to mature and proved very effective for assessing skills and team work. There was still some way to go in that some groups continued to agree in advance to mark all members equally. While having the value that this replicates real life situations, it was hard on the hard workers, unduly generous to the ineffective and indolent, while the inspired and industrious were not identified. However looking at the results, there were some grounds for suspecting that the model is not yet bias-free. Could Harriet just possibly have some other attributes not revealed by the assessment process which are affecting the results?

Learning from others

In parallel to our own growing pains and pleasures, other universities were facing up to similar problems of ensuring and demonstrating fairness and refining their techniques. From Sunderland University, Mark Lejk describes a number of approaches (Lejk 1994). Although he favours equal sharing of marks he is conscious of the resentment caused by the severely uncommitted and set up ground rules to deal with the situation. In the case of one or more team member not pulling their weight, the others can approach the tutor and request that this member is warned, and if the tutor agrees (obviously there must be a check to eliminate illness or other genuine reasons for lack of contribution) a 'yellow card' is issued. If the student does then start to measure up, then the card may be withdrawn, but if the team feels there has been insufficient improvement the student will have 20% deducted from the final team mark. If things deteriorate further then the tutor can issue a 'red card' which results in a mark of 0% for that student. In practice, the cards are invoked rarely (4 times out of 62 teams) but there was relief amongst students, a number of whom had had unpleasant experiences of team work, that there was a mechanism to address the problem. At the same time, the tutor felt the emphasis on team work was reinforced.

Case study of a maturing model

At Napier University, Goldfinch and Raeside (1990) were reporting their work on peer group assessment with mathematics students. It had many similarities to the Plymouth approach described above and illustrated in figure 1 - with the tutor allocating a mark to the group product; each student marking the other group members privately on the basis of their contribution to the assignment and the use of a two part questionnaire - Part 1 listing the tasks involved and Part 2 addressing the process skills.

Lessons from coming of age in peer assessment and group work

Part 1 (tasks) - a questionnaire was constructed in which for each of the tasks listed - the student who contributed most, could be identified and the number of times that student was mentioned was compared to the maximum possible number of mentions (where more than one individual was mentioned against task then each was awarded the appropriate fraction).

$$Part\ 1 = \frac{no.\ of\ mentions\ of\ individual}{possible\ no.\ of\ mentions}$$

Part 2 (skills) - lists a summary of the process skills carried out collectively during the project. Each student was required to award a mark between 0 and 4 to each group member (apart from themselves) to reflect the person's contribution to that part of the process. The mark is therefore the result of the sum of the actual marks awarded to that person divided by the highest possible score (ie 4 x total number of skills).

$$Part\ 2 = \frac{actual\ sum\ scored}{highest\ possible\ score}$$

As a result of these two calculations, each student would have an individual Peer Assessment score (PA score) and the individual's final mark would be derived from *(PA score) x (group mark)*.

Their model was mathematically more sophisticated - as one might expect from a mathematics department (for an example of how the calculation works - see Appendix A).

This approach seemed likely to offer improved reliability and we decided to apply it within civil engineering where team work, shared responsibility and communication across the group are all essential at every level of the profession (Rafiq & Fullerton 1996).

The project was a realistic scenario in which groups of four or five students had to respond to a project brief. They had to set up and attend regular project progress meetings, usually about half an hour following a scheduled lecture. Each group had to appoint a communicator who took notes of problems and discussed them with the tutor. They also had to keep a **project diary** which was an essential part of their project report and included reflections on professional practice. Specific tasks were identified by the group on their first meeting and allocated to individual group members these were noted in the diary along with summaries of discussions of each of the meetings. These summaries and current work were presented to the tutor at stages throughout the project, which ensured that the group kept to its target deadlines and allowed the tutor to guide and give formative feedback.

In all other respects, the Goldfinch and Raeside model was followed.

Part 2 worked well and students were relatively unbiased in their assessments of the group/team process (for an example the form the students completes see Appendix B).

Lessons from coming of age in peer assessment and group work

However, a number of problems were encountered with Part 1 of the procedure in that there was still resistance by students to marking each other's work in what appeared to them to be a subjective way and the tutor also felt that there was some bias. There was no opportunity to gauge the percentage contribution where more than one name was mentioned, and if one person's contributions were considerably higher than others, it was possible for them to score over 100%. In addition students had difficulty in recalling who did what, some time after the event.

To address these points it was decided to replace Part 1 with the project report and the project diaries in which the specific tasks that have been carried out are identified by the students themselves, who have also signed their own pieces of work. The diaries confirm the tutor's own assessment of the time and commitment spent by individuals on different tasks. This procedure in itself relates well to professional practice in the discipline, where there is always a detailed brief of every specified task, for its presentation, timescales and detail requirements.

This process has allowed the tutor to find ways fairly distributing marks to a group project and has increased transparency by giving both tutor and students an accurate checking mechanism. The diaries contribute significantly to the students' self -awareness and learning process, as does feedback on the particular part which the student did and can relate to the mark achieved for it. By bringing so much of the process to the attention of the students at an early stage, the assessment becomes 'front loaded' (Gibbs et al 1992) thus contrasting with earlier models where students didn't know the criteria until they had to complete the form at the end of the project.

Although students were not used to working in a framework of continuous deadlines, their initial reluctance was replaced by enthusiasm as they began to realise how it allowed them to experience the working patterns of their profession. In addition, they became more aware of their own responsibilities and their interdependence, so were motivated to complete their individual tasks on time and not 'let the side down'. They also learnt to support and encourage each other to keep up standards. They discovered that missed deadlines incur penalties (marks in HE; are equivalent to cash in the real world) and they improved their time management and avoided the usual last minute panics.

This case study demonstrated the organic nature of the growth and development of assessment and perhaps of peer assessment in particular. We found in Part 2 an 'off the shelf' approach which transferred easily and effectively to this and other disciplines. At the same time, we found that not all of others' techniques (ie Part 1) transfer well but that in this case it led to a development which benefited all parties. Monitoring and feeding back to groups instead of individuals significantly reduced the tutor's time. The process motivated the students, gave them added insight to their professional practice and significantly improved their task/time and personal management skills while developing and crediting their team work abilities.

Although the calculations sound cumbersome, they were done with a piece of computer programming by the subject lecturer (available on request from the University of Plymouth.)

Lesson eight - you never stop learning and colleagues in other institutions face similar problems and can contribute to solutions which may however need adaptation to a new context.

Lessons from coming of age in peer assessment and group work

If maturing is the point at which characteristics begin to settle, having learnt from early experimentation, explorations, and mistakes, having shared experienced with others and learnt from them and have reached a point of some self assurance - then this is now a fairly well-matured model. It has responded to its environment, which not only meets the challenge of increased student numbers and the call from employers for graduates who can work in teams with a range of transferable skills, but also demonstrates underpinning requirements for assessment:

- It is reliable - allocation of marks are evidenced in the project diaries and project reports.
- It is valid - it assesses the tasks and skills it sets out to measure.
- It is relevant - the skills and tasks are clearly seen by the students as appropriate to their profession.
- It is manageable - mathematical model enables quick calculation and sorting of student scores (with aid of a computer spreadsheet).
- It is transparent - the brief and criteria are clear and up front.
- It is formative as well as summative, contributing good feedback to the learning process.
- Above all - it is fair despite being an approach (group work) which is widely suspected and rejected on the grounds that it cannot bias free.

However maturity does not mean set for ever. Forever is forever changing anyway! For example our agenda now includes increased use of IT. Will future project diaries be emailed to the tutor? Will the meetings be 'virtual' with computer mediated conferencing? Will the developing work in progress be screen shared across the group on individual student's personal computers? Will the tutor 'drop in' on a group's video conference linking them from locations across the region? Will the external examiner be hovering around in cyberspace? As we strengthen our links with industry will the group have an industrial workplace mentor to relate to? Will some members of the group be dispersed around HE and industry not to mention the globe? Watch this space......

References

Fry, S. (1990) Implementing and evaluation of practice of peer marking in Higher Education *Assessment and Evaluation in Higher Education Vol 15 No 3*

Gibbs, G. (1992) *Teaching More Students No 4 Assessing More Students* (PCFC) Oxford

Goldfinch, J. M. & Raeside, R (1990) Development of peer assessment technique for obtaining individual marks on a group project, *Assessment and Evaluation in Higher Education Vol 15 No 3*, pp. 177 - 189

Lejk, M. (1994) Team Assessment - Win or Lose, *New Academic Vol 3 No3 Summer* SEDA Birmingham

Rafiq, Y. & Fullerton, H. (1996) Peer assessments of group projects in civil engineering, *Assessment and Evaluation in Higher Education*, Vol 21, No 1, pp. 69 - 81

Appendix A

Example of calculations involved in the Napier model

Table 1. Part 1 score

Name	Mentions 1	Mentions 2	Mentions 3	Mentions 4	Average	Part 1 Score
Bill	3.50		3.75	4.50	3.92	0.33
Ann	3.50	3.75		3.50	3.58	0.30
Heather	6.50	5.50	7.50		*6.50	0.54
Dave		3.50	3.50	3.75	3.58	0.30

Table 2. Part 2 score

Name	Mark 1	Mark 2	Mark 3 Score	Mark 4	Average	Part 2
Bill	22.00	9.50	20.00		17.20	0.54
Ann	22.00	10.50		20.00	17.50	0.55
Heather	22.00		23.00	23.00	22.70	0.71
Dave		11.00	19.00	21.00	17.00	0.53

Table 3.

Name	PA Score	Revised PA Score	Individual marks
Bill	0.47	0.92	55.00
Ann	0.47	0.92	55.00
Heather	0.65	1.27	76.00
Dave	0.45	0.88	53.00
Average	0.51		

Table 3 shows the final marks for the individuals in the group and the calculations below show how these were arrived at, with Heather's case used as an example. The original article had weighted the skills element as of the process and the group process as .

PA Score = [Part 1 score + Part 2 score]

Example: Heather's PA Score is $\frac{[(\times (0.54)] + [(2) \times (0.71)]}{3} = 0.65$

$$\text{Revised PA score} = \frac{\text{PA score}}{\text{Average PA score for that group}}$$

The average PA score for this group is 0.51 (as shown in Table 3).
Revised PA score for Heather = 0.65 / 0.51 = 1.27
The group project mark, assessed by the tutor, was 60%.
Therefore Heather's final mark is 1.27 (her revised PA score) x 60 (her group's mark) = 76%

Appendix B

Example of questionnaire form used by Civil Engineering at University of Plymouth

Peer Assessment Questionnaire
Assessment of others is an important skill, you should take time to answer these questions, forcing yourself to be objective and unbiased. Whilst completing this sheet, remember that the assessment you make is affecting your own mark as well as others.

Group: D   **Your name:** Dave
                         Name of group members   **Initials**

(1)   Heather   HR
(2)   Bill   BD
(3)   Ann   AC
(4)   Dave   DB

In this part, write *initial/s* of the major contributor/s.
Write one initial on each line.
If no one apart from yourself contributed much to that section write *'No one'*.
If everyone contributed equally write *'Everyone'*.
If there were two major contributors write both names.

Apart from yourself who (if any) in your group contributed most to:

1. General

- Planning and distribution of responsibilities   *HR*
- Suggesting assumptions and preliminary design ideas   *HR*
- Compiling and writing report   *HR, BD*
  (i.e. 50% of work attributed to Heather, 50% to Bill)

2. Design and checking of elements

- **Slab**
  - Design   *AC*
  - Check   *HR*

- **Beam**
  - Design   *HR*
  - Check   *BD*

- **Column**
  - Design   No one i.e. (Dave alone has done this)
  - Check   *AC*

Lessons from coming of age in peer assessment and group work

- **Footing**
  - Design **BD**
  - Check No one (i.e. Dave alone has done this)

3. **Detailing (Drawings and bar bending schedule)**

   General arrangements **HR**
   Slab **AC**
   Beam **HR**
   Column **AC**, No one (i.e. Ann + Dave have done this)
   Foundation **BD**

Group

Your name

Part 2

This part refers to the project as a whole. As a responsible member of the team you are asked to award marks from 0 to 4 according to the following scale, to each member of the team apart from yourself.

Scale

0 didn't contribute

1 willing but not successful

2 average

3 above average

4 outstanding

Put names of your group members here *Heather (HR), Bill (BD), Ann(AC) Dick (DB) Dave (DH)*

Names
Overall level of participation
Understanding what was required
Suggesting ideas
Extracting something useful from ideas
Performing routine tasks
Drawing things together (consolidation)
Keeping the group going in difficult patches
Sorting out problems

Totals

Peer assessment: and pitfalls

Leonora Ritter,
Charles Sturt University

I have always been strongly attracted to the option of peer assessment. It empowers students, gets them involved as agents in the assessment process, gives them valuable experience of evaluating and assessing and enhances their understanding of the assessment process. Experience, however, has taught that there are problems. Students do not always have a full enough comprehension of the assessment criteria being applied. They lack the knowledge and experience necessary to judge some criteria. They often lack the maturity and objectivity necessary when they are placed in a position of power, influencing the grades received by other students.

Effective use of peer assessment, then, seems to depend on ensuring their understanding of the criteria being applied and their competence to apply them and structuring the exercise in such a way as to minimise disabling or corrupting feelings of personal power.

I have used peer assessment in two very different ways, each of which has included strategies to minimise these problems. The first approach involved peer assessment of tutorial performance. This assessment contributed 25% to the final grade of the student who was assessed. The 'corrupting' effects of personal power were minimised by embedding the assessment in collective action. The assessment was carried out by every member of the tutorial group (average size 18).

Tutorial performance seemed a good area for peer assessment, as it was reasonable to assume that in judging the effectiveness of tutorial contribution, students were as competent as me. Furthermore, it seemed fair to the student being assessed to draw on more than one view. To further the student's feeling of empowerment, and ensure that they understood and could use the criteria that were applied, I allowed them to establish these criteria. The result was a three point check-list: participation, interest and enthusiasm and effectiveness of contribution. The evaluation process involved each student in the group anonymously annotating a class list with a grade for each member of the group against each criterion. The results were then averaged by simple arithmetic to produce a final collective participation grade for each individual.

The advantages of this assessment included assessing oral and interactive competencies not assessed by other methods; allowing those students who thought quickly, synthesised and expressed ideas well and had better oral than written expression to gain credit; encouraging and rewarding

rch; and penalising the idle, the bored, the boring, the ill-prepared and the ignorant.
ages included subjectivity; making some students nervous and penalising the shy
introvert and the slow but careful thinker; rewarding extroverts and disadvantaging
of a tutorial in which there were one or two very dominant personalities.

assessment increased student learning by developing understanding of the necessary
riteria and by enhancing their confidence in their right and ability to discriminate between peer contributions. By weighting this assessment at 25% of the total, students were empowered to significantly affect the results of their peers. Some colleagues have found that thus empowering students has made them too harsh. I found my group tended to err in the opposite direction. In comparison with my personal judgements of the students, the number of 'B' grades awarded by the group was almost identical, but peers awarded nearly twice as many 'A' grades as I did and 20% fewer 'C' grades than I did. This experiment was carried out at a time when I was working within a criterion-based grading system. The findings of my colleague's current experiment, that students are unacceptably harsh on each other, may be the result of the current competitive grading system in which student grades are often scaled to meet prescribed norms. Under this system, students can advantage themselves by marking others down. This clearly militates against effective summative peer assessment.

The most serious disadvantage was the time consumed in compiling the results of more than 60 students grading each other over three criteria (this experiment preceded the computer age). These time constraints, combined with growing discomfort about the equity of what might be actually being measured, led me eventually to drop this form of assessment. The main loss was the distancing of students from the assessment process.

Recently, I have revisited peer assessment, but in a different way and focusing on a different assessment task. I have introduced peer assessment of essays to give students the experience of judging each others work, to make them aware of the reader-in-the-essay and hopefully to thereby enhance their own essay writing. A key difference between this and many forms of peer assessment is that this peer assessment does not involve awarding a grade and does not contribute to the final grade of the one whose work is assessed by the peer. Rather, it is, in itself, assessed. This engages students in peer assessment in a way that requires them to do their best and makes them aware of the assessor's perspective, but does not risk unacceptable outcomes resulting from empowering inexperienced or emotionally involved markers. This is particularly an issue in the case of essays, which are a traditional form with well-established and widely recognised criteria. This form, a structured presentation of research and conclusions based on evidence, is an essential skill in the history discipline. My goal was to devise a strategy that involved students as peer assessors and enhanced the learning aspect of the essay writing process without jeopardising the traditional rigour of essays as a form of assessment.

I conducted an experimental approach to essay writing in two subjects in first semester 1997. The subjects were HST 207, History of Childhood, a second year subject with an enrolment of 59, and HST 105, Australian Studies History, a first year subject with an enrolment of 21. A number of strategies were used. These included:

Peer assessment: lessons and pitfalls

- having a peer evaluate each essay against a detailed list of criteria prior to submission so that the writer could benefit from peer criticism and possibly modify the essay before submission,
- evaluating a peer's essay against a detailed list of criteria prior to submission so that they would develop a sense of the-reader-in-the-essay and hone their critical faculties,

Other associated strategies involved:

- the absence of specific due dates to put students in control of their timing and help them learn time management,
- the explicit right to resubmit essays so that they could develop the product and learn from marker's feedback by applying it,
- the essay writer evaluating their own work against a detailed list of criteria prior to submission so that they would see their essay from a reader's perspective and evaluate it carefully before they handed it in,
- the marker marking the essay against a detailed list of criteria so that students could see exactly where problems occurred and where they were doing well,
- defining both ends of the spectrum on the list of criteria rather than making not good merely the opposite of good.
- and making the criteria available from the beginning of the semester.

Self and peer evaluations were requested in the following format:

> You MUST hand in two evaluation sheets with your essay on the first submission. One is to be filled in by you and one is to be filled in by another student doing the subject. These evaluations will not count towards the final grade of the essay but will be themselves evaluated. They are worth 10% each to the respective evaluators.

You must also ensure that you do an evaluation of another student's essay to be handed in with that essay. (This will be worth 10% to you).

It was made clear that the students were being marked in these exercises on their ability to critically evaluate what they read and that their assessment of their own or others work would not affect the grades awarded to the essays.

Students were provided with a detailed list of criteria to ensure that they were marking according to traditional standards. I emphasise that the goal was to enhance their performance and understanding in the task of writing traditional essays for which there are already well established criteria, so it did not seem useful to engage students in determining the criteria for this task. In the detailed list of criteria, all were described in qualitative terms with the best possible outcome on one side of a spectrum and worst outcome on the other. There was a deliberate attempt to avoid describing one side of the spectrum merely as the opposite of its partner (e.g. legible: illegible or argument develops: argument does not develop) so that students could understand more clearly what qualities were desirable and what qualities were undesirable in each case. Standards for judging each criterion were thus included in the description of the criterion:

Peer assessment: lessons and pitfalls

Column 1	A	B	C	D	Column 2
Legible, clearly set-out and carefully proof read	—	—	—	—	Difficult to read untidy, poorly spaced, typographical errors.
Based on wide reading, including specialist works	—	—	—	—	Sources too few and/or too general/ introductory.
Demonstrates thorough understanding of subject matter	—	—	—	—	Big gaps in knowledge.
All generalisations supported with evidence, example and/or authorities	—	—	—	—	Too many unsupported generalisations - why do you believe what you say?
Evidence evaluated. Expert opinion identified as such. Critical appraisal of sources value.	—	—	—	—	Treats all sources as of equal Confuses opinion, expert opinion and evidence.
Evidence is representative and sufficient.	—	—	—	—	Evidence too sparse, too selective or too general.
Discusses evidence to show how it supports the argument. Quotes only used to support or focus an argument.	—	—	—	—	Quotations used instead of argument. Expects data, examples etc to 'speak for themselves'.
Constructs an argument based on questioning and analysis.	—	—	—	—	Narrative/ descriptive, lacks explanation and interpretation.
Introduction reflects topic, clarifies standpoint and anticipates structure.	—	—	—	—	Introduction missing, too general, unfocussed, not relevant or does not foreshadow the essay.
Conclusion concise, resolves issues raised in the question.	—	—	—	—	Conclusion missing, unfocussed, inappropriate or too general.
Essay holds focus on topic. Discussion clearly directed, flows well from point to point.	—	—	—	—	Essay wanders from topic. Discussion is vague and general or too sporadic, links missing or unclear.
Argument develops.	—	—	—	—	Argument is repetitive or circular.
Each paragraph properly developed with a topic sentence to focus the reader.	—	—	—	—	Paragraphs unfocussed, lacking in structure or direction
Concise, fluent, clear and easy to follow.	—	—	—	—	Poor expression leaves reader lost and confused.

Peer assessment: lessons and pitfalls

Students were asked to evaluate their peers by ticking the relevant column. They were told:

A tick in column A means the comment in column 1 applies; column B means the comment in column 1 is more valid than the comment in column 2; column C means the comment in column 2 is more valid than the comment in column 1; column D means the comment in column 2 applies.

One problem that emerged was ensuring that every student both evaluated an essay and had a peer evaluate their essay. Some failed to attach a peer evaluation to their essay. I reminded them that this was necessary but in a few cases they seemed unable to find someone who would do it. Should you penalise a student for being unpopular? Similar problems were caused by students who failed to complete an evaluation. Four first years and five second years who completed all other requirements failed to meet this one.

A second related problem was the amount of marks attached to the task. 10% was probably too much of a loading. I would like to find a way of making them do it without attaching a mark. Making it necessary for them to meet terms is a possibility but an onerous one. What of the High Distinction student in everything else, who found this bit too hard to organise or failed to find a peer who would let them do it?

Another problem was the logistic of how to make things happen in the right order. In some cases, the peer read the essay and submitted it with the appraisal attached without the writer seeing the appraisal. This defeated the object of the exercise. Where the peer review was read it did not seem to affect the final work. If I continue with this aspect of the process, the mechanics of it will have to be reconsidered. I could go down the track of getting students to submit two essays, the draft before peer review and the final submission taking on board peer criticism. This would, however, significantly increase the marking load.

The difficulty of peer subjectivity remained in spite of the attempt to offset it by divorcing the peer judgement from the essay writer's final grade. The goal of learning to help someone else by being a constructively critical reader did not seem to be achieved. Only half of the sample did not find evaluating too difficult. A number of students commented to me that as peers they felt obliged to be generous. They understood that they would not affect the mark but did not want to hurt the essay writer's feelings. Notwithstanding this, 86% of second years and 71% of first years did not find being evaluated 'too difficult'.

The goal of enhancing essay writing through subjecting it to a peers scrutiny was partly achieved in the perception of the majority of the students. 67% of second years and 78% of first years found being evaluated 'helpful' or 'very helpful'.

The goal of having students experience the reader-in-the-essay was also achieved to some extent. About 70% of both groups said they definitely learned from the experience of reading another essay and another 21% in each group 'maybe' learned from it. 72% of second years and 79% of first years found evaluating another 'helpful' or 'very helpful'.

The detailed list of criteria was clearly the most significant of all the innovations. There were many expressions of appreciation, and, regrettably, contrasts with less favourable experiences in other subjects. More second years (67%) than first years (50%) found the detailed list of criteria easy to follow. In future, I shall try to set aside a time to work through it in detail early in the semester. Over 90% of both samples found the list 'helpful' or 'very helpful'.

Conclusion

This paper looks at two processes designed to increase students' participation in assessment:

- engaging students as assessors of their own and their peers' essays in order to involve them as partners in each other's learning and to improve their writing by making them aware of the reader-in-the-essay and
- the use of a detailed feedback sheet.

Both proved to have significant value for students.

My final reflection for the moment is that structural changes can only achieve so much. Real change must be accompanied by actively working with the new processes and only become effective as students develop new skills and as changes in attitude encompass the idea of assessment as part of the learning process rather than a series of hoops to be cleared. This will take time.

Summary of student feedback based on questionnaire responses.

HST 207 (History of Childhood) N=43; HST 105 (Australian Studies - History) N= 14.

Detailed list of criteria

	yes		maybe		no		don't know	
	207	105	207	105	207	105	207	105
Empowered by:	49%	57%	21%	43%	26%		5%	
Make feel anxious:	12%	14%	23%	14%	60%	71%	5%	
Learn from:	58%	57%	28%	21%		14%	12%	7%
Easy to follow:	67%	50%	23%	43%	2%	7%	9%	
How helpful:	v. helpful		helpful		made no difference		unhelpful	
	33%	36%	60%	57%	7%	7%		

Peer assessment: lessons and pitfalls

Evaluating another's essay

	yes		maybe		no		don't know	
	207	105	207	105	207	105	207	105
Make feel anxious:	47%	36%	16%	21%	37%	43%		
Too difficult:	9%	29%	37%	21%	53%	50%		
Learn from:	70%	71%	21%	21%	2%		7%	7%
How helpful:	v. helpful		helpful		made no difference		unhelpful	
	23%	29%	49%	50%	26%	14%	2%	7%

Having a peer evaluate your work

	yes		maybe		no		don't know	
	207	105	207	105	207	105	207	105
Make feel insecure:	16%	14%	35%	21%	44%	64%	2%	
Too difficult:	2%	7%	9%	21%	86%	71%		
Learn from:	47%	36%	30%	64%	14%		7%	
How helpful:	v. helpful		helpful		made no difference		unhelpful	
	18%	21%	49%	57%	26%	7%	5%	14%

Peer assessment - A construction "Tool"?

W D Sher and D R Twigg
Loughborough University

Background and summary

The construction industry is notoriously conservative. This, as well as the long recession experienced by the industry and the attractive career prospects of other courses has made it increasingly difficult to recruit students to construction. Publicising innovative teaching during open days is one method we have used to attract students to our degree programmes. In this context peer assessment is a technique we use and advertise to aspirant construction engineers and managers. This paper describes how we have incorporated peer assessment into our construction technology and surveying modules. There are three parts: the first describes a project to design and construct a reinforced concrete lintel; the second describes the coursework element of two engineering surveying modules where students are required to undertake library research, outdoor fieldwork and computer simulation exercises; and the third describes the lessons we have learnt and identifies some outstanding issues.

1 Construction technology

Overview of the project
The project was part of a module entitled Building Technology (Framed Structures) which is taken by second year students studying for undergraduate degrees in Construction Engineering Management (CEM), Commercial Management and Quantity Surveying (CMQS) and third year Masters students in Civil and Building Engineering (MEng). This module continues the theme of building technology from early years of study and exposes students to the technology of large, complex buildings. In practice, graduates from these disciplines are involved in the design, construction, costing and management of building and civil engineering projects. The overall aim of the project is to provide a task which exposes students to the challenges and inter-disciplinary conflicts experienced on construction sites. As such, the project provides students with "hands-on" experience in the various roles that they will be expected to fulfill upon graduation. These include structural design, specification writing, temporary works design, measurement, planning, construction, quality control and testing. In addition, the project exposes students to "real-life" issues of coordination, communication and conciliation.

The project contributes 12.5% (half of the coursework component) of the module mark and involves:

- the design of a reinforced concrete lintel

- the production of briefing documents to facilitate its construction

- peer assessment of the design (including the briefing documents)

- the design of temporary works necessary for the construction of the lintels

- the construction of the lintels based on the designs

- peer assessment of lintel construction

- structural testing of the lintels

The project was delivered to a large group of students (ranging from sixty to seventy students). To accommodate this number and to simulate a "real life" experience, all work was done in groups of three or four. Students chose their own group members and then proceeded to design the lintels. The resulting documentation was then handed to another group who built a lintel according to this design documentation. A flow chart of this sequence of operations is given in Figure 1. (p. 89). This shows how documents were passed between groups so that work could progress and also shows the points at which assessment was completed.

How we planned to run the project

In devising the project, we arranged for the following to occur:

- Students would hand in their completed designs to their tutors. These designs needed to take into account:

  (i)   how strong the lintel needed to be
  (ii) how it was to be built into the external wall of a brick house
  (iii) how to maintain the weatherproofing and visual characteristics of the external wall

- We would allocate each set of design documentation to another group

- Groups would then be asked to assess the design efforts of their peers in terms of criteria the class had established by consensus at an earlier stage. Figure 2 (p.90) provides a sample page of the assessment sheets used.

Peer assessment - A construction "Tool"?

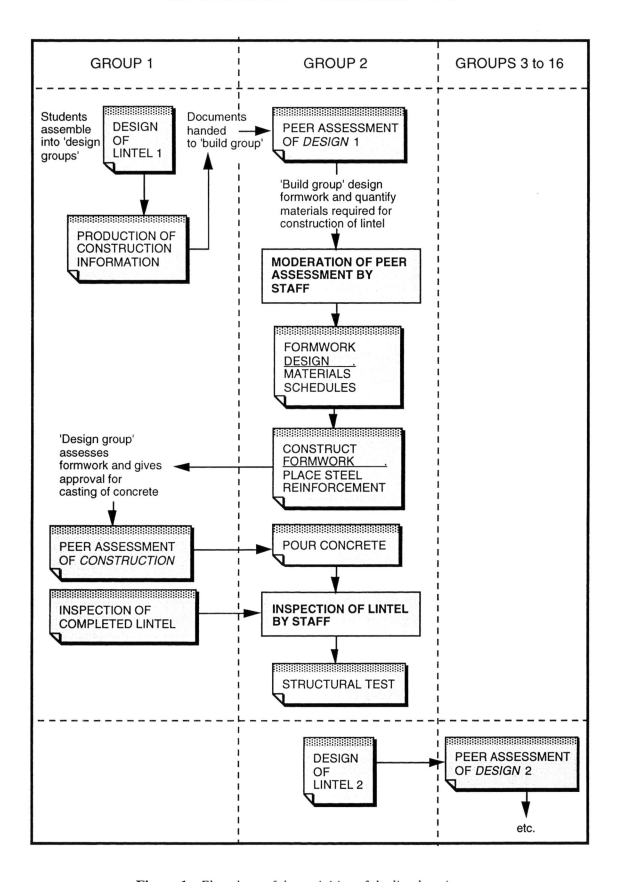

Figure 1: *Flowchart of the activities of the lintel project*

Assessment of Lintel Design
(Design Worth 70% of the O/A Lintel Coursework)

Group No. being assessed ....
Group No. doing assessment ....

1   CLARITY/PRESENTATION (20%)   %
1.1   The text/calculations was clear and unambiguous
      POOR   Average   Excellent
      0-1% 2-4%   7-8%

1.2   Sketches were included and were well drawn, clear and consistent with the text
      POOR   Average   Excellent
      0-1% 2-4%   7-8%

2   BUILDABILITY (20%)
2.1   All aspects of the design of the lintel itself applied good principles of buildability
      POOR   Average   Excellent
      0-1% 2-4%   7-8%

2.2   All aspects of the brick/block detailing applied good principles of buildability
      POOR   Average   Excellent
      0-1% 2-4%   7-8%

3   BRICK DESIGN/DETAILING (15%)
3.1   The brick/block aspects met the brief and relevant Building Regs.
      POOR   Average   Excellent
      0-1% 2-4%   7-8%

3.2   Issues such as cavity drainage, brick support, external brick appearance etc. have been
      well covered
      POOR   Average   Excellent
      0-1% 2-4%   7-8%

4   CONCRETE MIX DESIGN (15%)
4.1   Calculations are accurate and assumptions correct
      POOR   Average   Excellent
      0-1% 2-4%   7-8%

Figure 2: *Sample of the design assessment sheet*

Peer assessment - A construction "Tool"?

- All groups would then take on the role of construction contractors and would quantify the materials needed for the construction of their lintel. This would involve them in formwork (or "temporary works") design as they would have to consider how to construct a mould capable of containing and supporting wet concrete.

- We would then ask students to prepare a list of the materials they required to build their lintels. These lists would then be handed to our laboratory technicians who would purchase and cut the materials to the sizes required.

- Students would then assemble their formwork, fix their reinforcement and call on their designers to approve their work (This procedure mirrors the practice on construction sites where consultant engineers generally check on the quality of formwork and inspect the positioning and quantity of reinforcement before concrete is placed). To formalise this approval, an assessment sheet (similar to that shown in Figure 2) would be completed by the design teams.

- Once this second assessment had been completed, the construct groups would mix and place concrete according to the designers specifications and leave the lintels suitably protected so that the concrete could set. After an appropriate time, construct groups would remove the formwork from the hardened concrete.

- At this stage, design groups would carry out a further visual inspection of the completed lintels.

- After an appropriate curing period, the lintels would be placed in a test rig and loads applied to simulate site conditions. Plate 1 shows one of the lintels during testing.

Plate 1: One of the lintels during testing

- The marks for the project were made up as follows:

DESIGN

Design	65%
Achievement of design loads	5%

CONSTRUCT

Construction	15%
Cutting list	10%
Quality (determined by 'as-built' inspection)	5%

All these activities were spread over two terms. A programme indicating this is given in Figure 3.

Wk No	Activity	Deadline
1	Concept/shape design	
2	Concept/shape design	
3	Reinforcement design	Develop assessment criteria
4	Reinforcement design	
5	Concrete mix design	
6	Concrete mix design	Design work complete *SWAP DESIGNS*
7	Formwork design	
8	Formwork design & Cutting List	Submit List BY END OF WEEK
9&10	STUDY BREAK & EXAMS	
11 to 17	Formwork and reinforcement assembly	
12 to 18	Cast concrete	
19	Test lintels and review	
20	EXAMS	

Figure 3: *Programme of the project*

What actually happened

Not all aspects of the project proceeded according to plan. The main differences from our proposals were:

- Construct groups had difficulty arranging meetings with design groups to approve their formwork and reinforcement. We had intentionally arranged for design documents to be handed from group to group in a "roll-on" manner to avoid problems of victimisation occurring in the peer assessment exercises (For example, Figure 1 shows that group two built group one's design but had their design built by group three, and so on). However, this approach proved complex - especially as three different student courses were involved (i.e. CEM, CMQS and MEng). Consequently some construct groups cast their lintels without the sanction of their designers - a problem particularly prevalent with multi-disciplinary groups. This had obvious implications for peer assessment and in these instances, we took our moderated marks (as described below) in place of the missing marks. It is interesting to note that arranging inspections by designers in real-life often also causes problems!

- In the case of those construct groups whose designers had failed to assess their efforts before casting concrete, we ended up marking the visual aspects of the lintels (in much the same way as a "clerk-of-works" on a construction site would do).

- We saw the task of producing a list of the materials required to construct the lintels as a relatively trivial part of the project. Some of our students obviously viewed this task in the same light and paid scant attention to it! Our technicians suffered the consequences as, in some cases, they had difficulty interpreting students' requirements. The assessment of this aspect was subsequently omitted.

- Some of the final visual inspections were not done by the students. Again, this had obvious consequences for peer assessment.

- A mechanical breakdown of our testing apparatus meant that testing of the lintels was not carried out with all students present.

- The marking scheme described above was modified to accommodate the problems described here.

It is hard to determine the extent to which these problems affected the project. We would argue that having things not go according to plan reflects everyday conditions on a construction site and, in this context, the problems experienced could be viewed to have added value to the project.

Evaluation

Staff and students had different reactions to the project and the peer assessment exercises.

1   Reaction of students

Open revolt! (... at least initially.) Most second year students came to appreciate the value of the project and the assessment exercises. However there was some general discontent and apprehension. Some of the reasons for this we identified as:

- *Unease at marking a colleague's work*
  Students felt ill-equipped and worried about assessing the work of their colleagues. This was especially true of the MEng students who, being in the third year of their studies, were understandably more concerned about passing or failing than other students (This is mainly due to the increased weighting of third year marks towards the class of their degree).
- *Fears of being victimised*
  Some students felt that they would be penalised if they marked down other students efforts. We had anticipated this problem and tried to avoid it - as already described. However, we did experience a case where a design group felt aggrieved at the design mark they had received and subsequently appeared to penalise their construct group's efforts. As these marks were moderated, cases such as these resulted in the peer assessed mark being adjusted accordingly.
- *Not wanting the responsibility of assessment*
  This was especially true of the MEng students - who had not been exposed to peer assessment before.

- *Being uncertain of the standard required*

  The scales ranging from POOR to EXCELLENT which we provided on our assessment sheets, (see Figure 2), presented some students with problems. To guide them in using this scheme, we provided hand-outs which described what we considered to be EXCELLENT, AVERAGE and POOR work (see Figure 4). Notwithstanding this, students still felt ill-equipped to assess the efforts of their peers.

To receive an **EXCELLENT MARK** for any of the criteria, your submission should include:

- **Summary information** that describes what you set out to do, how you did it, what your results were, any problems you encountered along the way and how you overcame them.
- Detailed information to back up the above. This would be logically set out with explanatory notes and sketches where appropriate. Your English would be clear and unambiguous and to the point.

To receive an **AVERAGE MARK** your submission would include:

- Some **summary information**
- **Detailed information** (as described above - but not quite as logically set out or as comprehensive). There may be some waffle or 'flowery' language and/or explanations and sketches that were not relevant.

To receive an **POOR MARK** you would have included:

- No (or very little) **summary information**
- Some **detailed information** but it would be difficult to follow, leave out areas and/or include a lot of waffle. Few sketches would have been provided and readers would be left wondering whether you really knew what you were talking about.

Figure 4: *Information provided to students to assist in completing peer assessment forms*

- *Skeptical of lecturer's motivation*

  Although no student actually voiced this fear, we were concerned that they felt we were only using peer assessment as a means of reducing our workload or because we couldn't be bothered to mark their efforts ourselves.

2   Reaction of staff

We were generally happy with the way the project and the assessment exercises progressed. We are fortunate in that most of the staff involved with our course support innovation but the situation could clearly be different. It is probable that not all staff in our department support the approach we have experimented with here.

3   Benefits to students

- *Taking responsibility*

The student groups had to take responsibility for considerably more aspects and activities than would be the case for a typical project in our department. We consider this to be a positive and developmental feature of the exercise.

Peer assessment - A construction "Tool"?

- ***Real-life situation***

The project provided a "real life" experience of some of the challenges and problems encountered in the construction industry. Although few students had worked in the industry, they were able to relate to the task in hand and generally enjoyed the work. A point not readily appreciated by some students was that the conflicts they experienced with their peers were similar to those they were likely to encounter in the workplace.

- ***Student interaction***

The nature of the project meant that students had to interact and solve organisational as well as technical problems. Furthermore, in the assessment process consensus had to be reached, requiring the groups to learn to accommodate different views and come to a decision.

- ***An opportunity to develop skills in evaluating other students' efforts***

We saw this as a key aspect of students' development. All those participating are likely to work in management roles and need to be able to judge the efforts of those they work with. This project is a tentative step towards tertiary education developing these skills. In addition, an appreciation of quality and the skill of developing quality consciousness is essential for construction professionals.

- ***Formative assessment***

Few current coursework projects in our department provide an opportunity for formative assessment. We see the fact that this project provides this chance as a positive aspect of the overall project. A detailed discussion on the benefits of formative assessment is provided in Brown and Knight (1994)

4 Benefits to staff

- ***Saving staff time***

We had hoped that student participation in assessment would reduce the time we spent marking. This was not the case - but it was also the first time we had tried peer assessment on this scale. On the subsequent occasion we ran this project, assessment was more streamlined, but our experience with a project of this nature is that peer assessment does not necessarily reduce staff time.

- ***Potential long-term benefit of less drudgery in marking***

Our involvement in peer assessment meant that we spent more time discussing the project and the results with the students and less time sitting on our own marking similar scripts. This interactive approach significantly reduced the drudgery normally associated with tutor assessment of large groups. However, we did spend some time on unnecessary tasks such as cajoling students to complete the practical aspects of their work in their allotted laboratory time slots.

- ***Early awareness of ambiguities / problems in coursework***

As a result of our close contact with students, we became aware of ambiguities in the wording of our brief and in the nature of the problems we had set. This feedback would have been difficult to obtain in a traditional environment.

- ***Opportunity to develop new ideas for coursework enhancement***

On more than one occasion, the comments and questions of students made us feel "Why didn't I ask that?" or "They didn't really appreciate what I was after - next time I'll phrase the question like this...". There are no doubt other situations where this kind of feedback is available but we felt that this was a valuable by-product of peer assessment.

- *Getting to know students better*

The close contact we were able to have with student groups enabled us to get to know them both as individuals and in a group environment.

What have we changed?

We have repeated this exercise and have refined some aspects. The following are the main issues we addressed:

- *Rely less on students to choosing the basis for assessment*

As already mentioned, we allowed students to choose the criteria for assessing their work. We reviewed these criteria and drew up the assessment sheets referred to earlier. With hindsight, we should also have marked a project as a "dry-run" to test the criteria as, in some cases, we found that groups interpreted aspects differently. We were probably too keen to mirror the criteria suggested by the students rather than rationalising them.

- *Influence the composition of groups*

We allowed students to choose their own group members. This resulted in most groups being drawn from one discipline (i.e. construction management, quantity surveying or civil engineering) as students preferred to work with their friends. This situation does not reflect conditions in the construction industry where the design (or construct) team on a project is seldom the same for another project. We have subsequently allocated students to groups ourselves though this has resulted in students finding it difficult to make and maintain contact with their group members.

- *Moderate more*

We had hoped to spend minimal time on moderation. Our intention was simply to review the assessment sheets, the completed lintels and the results of the tests on the lintels and adjust final marks as and where necessary. Again, with hindsight, we should have spent more time on this aspect.

- *Make the assessment sheets simpler*

The sheets we drew up (as shown in Figure 2) provided a range of marks for each criterion. Our intention was for students to complete all the necessary arithmetic. This proved unsatisfactory as students were distracted by these marks. We modified these sheets to provide grade descriptors, and completed the necessary arithmetic ourselves as a separate exercise.

- *Plan to minimise victimisation*

Some students expressed fears about being victimised by their peers. As already mentioned, this did appear to affect one group. To discourage this, we included a section in our revised assessment sheets which required assessors to justify the category allocated.

- *Provide examples of excellent work*

As already mentioned, students found it difficult to rate work in the categories provided in our assessment sheets. To address this, we subsequently provided examples of excellent work. This meant that, prior to our peer assessment meetings, we looked through all submissions and identified a good (but not necessarily the best) project. We then provided this anonymously as an benchmark. This proved successful in that students felt more confident in making their assessments.

2   Enginering surveying

Peer assessment has been used for two years in engineering surveying modules taken by students on the BEng and MEng Civil Engineering programmes. Surveying 2 is a compulsory module for all second year students and is taken by 80 to 100 students. Surveying at this level is a "hands-on" practical subject and all students are also required to attend a separate field course. The coursework element contributes only 20% towards the module assessment and is designed to give an alternative to the usual fieldwork exercises. By contrast, Surveying 3 is an optional third year module and is usually chosen by between 12 and 24 students, some of whom are on a full-time programme and others who have one year's experience in industry. The coursework element of this final year module contributes 50% towards the module assessment. Students are required to report on calibration fieldwork and computer simulation exercises.

Surveying 2 Coursework Requirements

Students are asked to work in self-chosen groups of four from their larger tutorial group and are required to:
- investigate a topic allocated by the staff teaching the module
- prepare an oral presentation on the topic to be given to the whole of their tutorial group and which should last for eight minutes followed by two minutes for questions
- prepare a two page handout to accompany the talk.

The topics allocated complement subjects covered in the lecture programme and require students to obtain information from relevant current journals rather than from the appropriate textbooks. Topics that have been used in the past include:
- Applications of lasers on construction sites
- The use of Digital Terrain Modelling packages in engineering surveying and design
- Technology and techniques of Global Positioning Systems surveying
- The checking and calibration of Electronic Distance Measurement (EDM) instruments
- Quality Assurance for surveying companies
- The role of photogrammetry in engineering surveying
- Principles and applications of the gyro-theodolite
- Principles and applications of Industrial Measuring Systems

After a four-week preparation period, each of the oral presentations and handouts is assessed by staff and by all peer groups in the relevant tutorial group. Students are asked to assess each presentation on:

Content (40%)	amount and relevance of information presented in talk (20%) and handout (20%)
Structure (30%)	clarity and organisation of material presented in talk (15%) and handout (15%)
Presentation (30%)	quality of delivery (10%), visual aids (10%) and handout (10%)

Peer assessment - A construction "Tool"?

Because students at this level are unsure about their ability to assess their colleagues work, a pro-forma assessment sheet is used (see Figure 5). As this sheet is distributed with the initial coursework briefing, it has the added advantage that it helps each group of students in preparing their own presentation.

In addition to the staff and peer assessment, each group is asked to assess its own effectiveness by completing a questionnaire and awarding a grade. The mean staff, mean peer and self assessment marks are weighted in the ratio 60:30:10 to give a final mark. To allow for any unequal contribution to the group effort, students are also asked to indicate on the self-assessment sheet what percentage (0 to 100%) of the final mark each individual member of the group should be awarded.

Surveying 3 Coursework Requirements

Once again students are asked to work in self-chosen groups. Given the much smaller overall student population each individual group usually has three members. The coursework amounts to 50% of the module assessment and requires each student group to undertake three exercises:

- determining the accuracy in use of theodolites or levels using British Standard procedures
- calibration of EDM instruments using a multi-station baseline
- design of a surveying network by computer simulation

The results of the practical work are delivered as reports, oral presentations or poster presentations. Each group has to adapt the information gained to the three styles of presentation used:

- the *report* is to be written in the style of a paper to be submitted to a named professional journal and has to have a maximum word-processed length of six sides of A4, including all graphics.
- the *poster* has to be an attractive A1 presentation.
- the *oral presentation* is to the whole option group and lasts for ten minutes followed by a few minutes for questions. A two-page handout also needs to be produced to accompany the talk.

Although the report is assessed by staff only, (to allay student fears of too much peer assessment for 50% of a module in the final year of their programme), peer assessment is used for both the oral and poster presentations. The format of the assessment is similar to that used in Surveying 2 and includes:

- the use of assessment pro-formas similar to Figure 5
- self assessment of group effectiveness
- the weighting of staff, peer and self assessment marks in the ratio 60:40:10 to give a final mark
- allowance for individual contribution to group effort

Peer assessment - A construction "Tool"?

Evaluation

The major advantages of introducing peer assessment into the Surveying 2 and Surveying 3 modules have been to:

- add variety to the coursework
- keep students alert during the presentations
- make students feel involved in the assessment process
- improve students own work by a more thorough appreciation of assessment details
- reduce the overall staff assessment time

However, there have also been some concerns. Initially, students are apprehensive that they are not trained to assess and they also fear that personalities will play a part in the assessment process and marks could be downgraded by other groups. The initial staff concerns were that the students would not treat the assessment seriously and that they would not be prepared to give low marks.

In order to test these concerns, the results of the peer assessment for both the modules described above for the two academic years in which it has been used have been analysed. A plot of the mean staff mark against the mean student mark awarded for each presentation is given in Figure 6 for Surveying 2 and in Figure 7 for Surveying 3. Although there is the expected scatter of results, it can be seen that there is a strong correlation between the marks awarded. This is particularly noticeable for Surveying 3. The students are obviously as adept as members of staff at recognising good, mediocre or poor work. Perhaps what is surprising is that, contrary to staff expectations, students appear reluctant to award high marks. With Surveying 2 for example, staff awarded 14 marks of 70% or above whereas students only awarded two such marks.

Another view of the peer marks awarded is given in Figures 8 and 9. These show plots of the average mark received by each group against the average mark given by each group. Unlike the previous plots, these show negative correlation, (quite strongly in the case of Surveying 3). The student mark awarded is thus determined by the perception of another groups work relative to their own: students who have produced good work give relatively low marks and vice versa.

One final look at more detailed marks is given in Figure 10. This shows all the marks awarded in Surveying 2 in the academic year 1996-97. It can be seen that although there is good overall correlation between staff, student and staff/student marks, there can be a wide variation of marks in individual cases. The two staff marks for Group A5, for example, differ by 13%. It is also interesting to note that there is one (and only one) possible case of a group underscoring another i.e. Group A1 were awarded 9 marks ranging from 66 to 79 and one of just 50.

Surveying 2 - Seminar Assessment Sheet

Assessment of Group .... by ....

Assessment Grades to be used

Grade	Description	Mark Range	Grade	Description	Mark Range
A*	Excellent	80-100%	D	Poor	40-49%
A	Very Good	70-79%	E	Very Poor	30-39%
B	Good	60-69%	F	Unsatisfactory	0-29%
C	Satisfactory	50-59%	Z	Not Submitted	0%
				Comments	Grade Awarded

Content (40%)	**Talk** (20%)	ie amount and relevance eg A* - just right amount and all very relevant or F - far too much/little and mostly irrelevant
	Handout (20%)	ditto
Structure (30%)	**Talk** (15%)	ie clarity and organisation eg A* - very clear and easy to follow or F - very difficult to follow
	Handout (15%)	ditto
Presentation (30%)	**Talk** (10%)	ie quality of delivery eg A* - very clearly audible, speed just right and lively varied tone or F - almost inaudible, far too fast/slow and very monotonous
	Visual Aids (10%)	ie quality eg A* - very clear and attractive or F - almost illegible
	Handout (10%)	ie quality eg A* - very clear and attractive or F - almost illegible

Figure 5: *Assessment sheet used for Surveying 2*

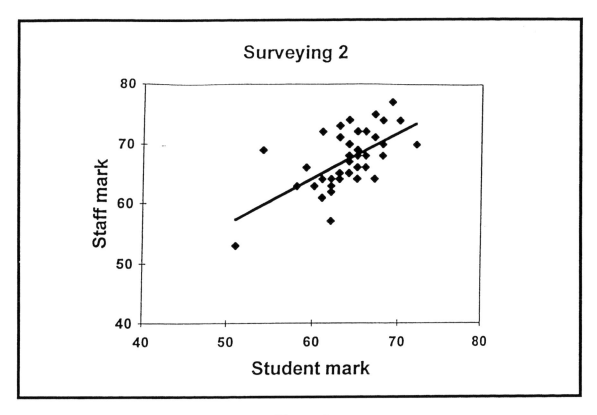

Figure 6

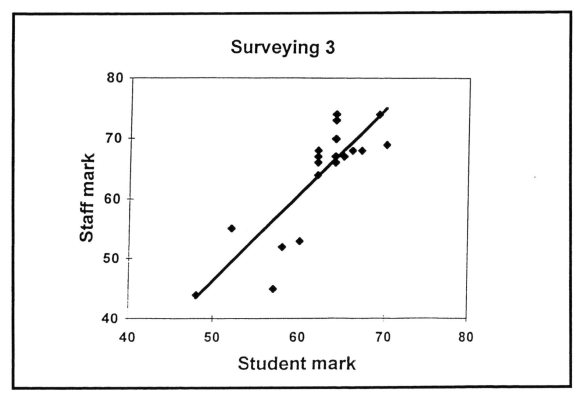

Figure 7

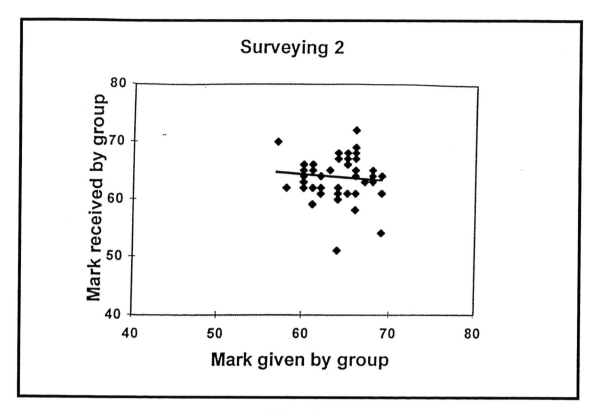

Figure 8

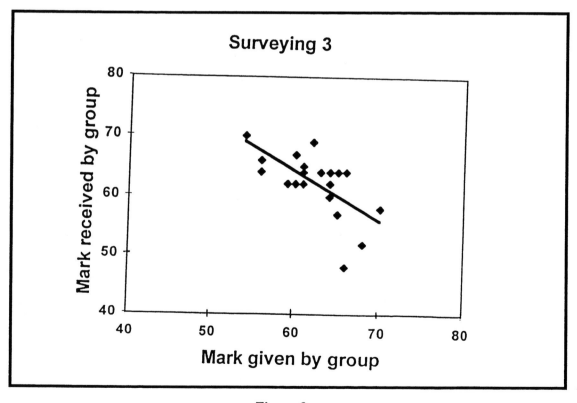

Figure 9

Peer assessment - A construction "Tool"?

Surveying 2 1996-97

	Staff 1	Staff 2	A1	A2	A3	A4	A5	A6	A7	A8	A9	staff 0.6	peer 0.3	self 0.1	total
A1	79	68		70	74	50	75	73	69	69	66	74	68	83	73
A2	63	65	70		63	65	68	70	63	69	65	64	67	90	67
A3	63	64	61	63		60	71	60	64	65	56	64	63	75	64
A4	54	60	55	58	68		68	62	66	57	60	57	62	65	59
A5	64	77	64	63	63	62		63	67	63	62	71	63	75	69
A6	74	70	67	71	63	66	62		61	68	62	72	65	75	70
A7	65	70	70	70	70	66		70		65	63	68	68	75	68
A8	67	65	67	62	70	64	71	67	63		65	66	66	75	67
A9	57	64	65	60	63	56	58	63	59	60		61	61	65	61

	Staff 1	Staff 2	B1	B2	B3	B4	B5	B6	B7	B8	staff 0.6	peer 0.3	self 0.1	total
B1	62	61		60	53	72	67	62	61	60	62	62	65	62
B2	70	70	62		60	64	65	66	65	63	70	64	90	70
B3	70	62	58	61		64	58	62	52	60	66	59	90	66
B4	63	64	54	60	61		65	65	59	61	64	61	75	64
B5	60	66	60	55	58	67		60	57	63	63	60	70	63
B6	63	68	72	61	64	69	67		55	64	66	65	75	66
B7	61	67	55	65	66	59	63	62		63	64	62	75	64
B8	59	69	59	57	66	60	63	66			64	62	75	64

	Staff 1	Staff 2	C1	C2	C3	C4	C5	C6	C7	C8	staff 0.6	peer 0.3	self 0.1	total
C1	74	69		70	65	69	65	60	67	63	72	66	75	70
C2	66	64	64		59	68	66	64	64	61	65	64	75	66
C3	68	65	64	67		67	59	59	68	65	67	64	75	67
C4	64	66	64	64	61		66	63	61	63	65	63	65	64
C5	61	66	65	67	60	65		55	59	59	64	61	65	63
C6	69	68	64	68	61	69	62		69	63	69	65	75	68
C7	78	71	68	71	67	65	64	65		66	75	67	75	72
C8	68	67	65	66	64	71	64		61		68	65	75	68

Figure 10: *Marks awarded in surveying 2 for 1996-7*

3 Lessons, outstanding issues and conclusions

Lessons we have learnt

The following observations are distilled from our experiences of peer assessment in the case studies of construction technology and surveying described above:

- *Start peer assessment as early as possible*
  Students' attitudes to assessment appear to harden during their academic career. We found students to be more receptive to the novel aspects of peer assessment in the earlier years of studies than third and final year students. Other peer assessment exercises that we have done with first year students have confirmed to us that peer assessment needs to be incorporated into the assessment culture of a degree course at an early stage in students' careers if it is to be successful.
- *Keep it simple*
  An overriding principle we have learnt is the need to keep things simple. In particular, areas that proved complex in the lintel project were the assessment sheets and the "roll-on" system of passing documentation from one group to another.
- *Stress the formative aspects of assessment*
  Students need to be made aware of the objectives of peer assessment. In some instances, we did not do this effectively and had to brief students at later stages. Once this was done we found them generally more receptive and co-operative.
- *Commit time up front and in the open*
  Students need to be made aware of the time and effort staff have put into preparing a project. This is, no doubt, true for all projects but it is especially so for those incorporating peer assessment. As already mentioned, students may feel that staff are primarily interested in reducing their own work load and that students will suffer by having to spend time marking work.
- *Brief students in detail*
  This is an essential ingredient. With project such as the lintel coursework, students need to be made aware of many issues and this cannot always be adequately explained in a hand-out.
- *Moderate marks*
  It is apparent that few students feel that their peers were competent to assess their work. This may be due to the fact that those we were involved with had minimal experience of peer assessment. However, it is essential that students see staff as being involved in the assessment process if these fears are to be alleviated. Moderation of marks is one way for this to occur.

What remains to be resolved?

We have not solved all the problems of peer assessment. Indeed, our collective list of things to do has grown considerably since we started. Some of the issues which we intend to concentrate on in the future include:

- *How to keep assessment simple but also comprehensive*
  The time allowed for peer assessment is restricted and needs to be used effectively. If this pressure is responded to by making assessment superficial, the whole exercise becomes a farce. Clearly it needs to be simple and effective.

- *How to moderate effectively without removing the benefit of peer assessment altogether*
  There may be conflict between peer assessment and staff moderation. An element of moderation is essential if staff are to remain in control and if Universities' regulations are to be upheld in terms of assessment of work that counts towards the grades of degrees awarded to students.
- *How to avoid victimisation difficulties*
  How do we avoid groups being victimised? Clearly this is an issue, but we have found that instances of victimisation are relatively easily identified.
- *How to deal with mixed classes*
  How do we deal with students that have no experience of peer assessment - especially when they are nearing the end of their undergraduate career?
- *How to influence conservative members of staff*
  How do we promote an accepting approach to peer assessment by conservative members of staff?

Conclusions

Notwithstanding the issues still to be addressed, we are positive about peer assessment. Used imaginatively, it provides a tool whereby construction students may be exposed to the realities of the commercial world whilst still at university. Peer assessment, linked with real-life simulation in a coursework exercise such as the lintel project is worth the effort to both staff and students. It is also promotes student interest in group presentations and encourages discussion on these occasions. We have found that some of the anticipated benefits of peer assessment (such as saving tutor's time) are not always realised but that other benefits make this approach worthwhile. Similarly, we have found that some of the perceived problems, such as victimisation, are relatively easily identified and addressed. We will continue to use peer assessment as a method of preparing students for careers in their chosen field - the construction industry.

References

Brown, S. and Knight, P. *Assessing learners in higher education*. Kogan Page, London (1994).

What do students think about peer assessment?

Sally Brown, Kay Sambell and Liz McDowell,
University of Northumbria at Newcastle

This paper describes the "Impact of Assessment" project at the University of Northumbria and uses students' own words to describe the process of peer assessment. Data collection for the project was undertaken between 1994 and 1997, to explore through a series of thirteen case studies of assessment in practice what students and staff thought about innovative assessment. The work primarily involved holding semi-structured interviews with groups of students on programmes where we had identified that innovative assessment practices were being implemented. We also interviewed the staff who assessed them, observed some of the sessions in which students were briefed or assessed, and examined documentary evidence such as assessment criteria , student handbooks, briefing sheets and so on.

Of course, what might be regarded innovative in some contexts will be old hat in others, but our definition took as its basis a view that innovative assessment implied a change in assessment practices from what was undertaken before in a particular context. These included means other than time-constrained unseen examinations, conventional tutor-marked essays and such like. We looked instead for instances of, for example, oral assessments, portfolios, poster assessments, live projects, group assessments and open-book examinations. In quite a number of our cases, we found that peer assessment was used where innovative assessment instruments were involved. Disciplines in our studies which involved peer assessment included Modern Languages, Geography, Business studies, Built Environment, Design, Electronic and Electrical Engineering, Psychology and Computer science

Our aim was to discover whether what we believed to be the case was demonstrated in practice: that students who had the opportunity to be assessed in innovative ways benefited from the process. We wanted to know whether their learning was deeper, whether assessment became integral to learning and whether tutors derived benefits as well. Our research led us to believe, as others in this volume have also suggested, that peer assessment is far from problematic, that there are a number of serious organisational issues associated with it that need to be solved if it is to work well, but that on the whole, it is worth persevering with.

What do students think about peer assessment?

Our interview data proved fascinating. Elsewhere we have written (and spoken) in more detail about the outcomes of the project but here we wish to focus specifically on peer assessment and what students had to say about it compared to the other kinds of assessment that they had experienced.

Our respondents were in no doubt that traditional exams were not from their perspectives good vehicles for learning:

> *"Exams test your ability to pass exams, rather than your knowledge of the subject."*

> *"The results you get are not just dependent on what you know, but on how good you are at doing exams."*

> *"You think "Just let me remember this for the next hour and a half." Then you don't care."*

> *"You shallow learn for an exam, but you don't know the stuff. It's poor learning, which you quickly forget."*

Many supporters of traditional forms of assessment, such as exams, uphold them as being exemplars of sound practice, contradicting the views of some of the students we talked to. Students in our sample saw exams as being unfair, (contrary to what most tutors think), since they aren't seen as a real test of learning, providing instead incentives to gamble on questions that might come up, rather than encouraging coverage of the whole curriculum:

> *"In normal exams you learn a whole essay and it doesn't come up, so it seems to the examiners that you know nothing."*

Innovative assessment methods, by contrast, were seen to reward consistent application and enable students to make the most of assessment opportunities:

> *"You can show you actually know the subject and you understand things. You usually get reward for the effort you put in."*

> *"I think [alternative assessment] gives a much better indication of what you know. It gives you much more chance to express your ideas. You can actually put more into your work and promote yourself into your work. You can certainly demonstrate how much more you know, or how you can interpret things."*

Students are often unhappy with traditional assessment methods that donít give them opportunities for remediation:

> *"I feel that exams are a big sort of hindrance. They really cause me severe problems because they're one-off. With continuous assessment, say I get a bad mark, I can improve on that next week and I can see where I've made my cock-ups today and work it all out. If you do make one disaster, it doesn't affect the whole thing."*

What do students think about peer assessment?

They also express concern that it is possible to get marks without ever really getting to grips with the work. This student is talking about the benefits of being involved in his own assessment as opposed to having the tutor mark it, where he felt he never really engaged with the subject:

> "I did all the graphs and I seemed to have got most of it right but I knew myself that I didn't understand what I was doing all of the time I knew I didn't understand what I was doing. The graphs were no problem, ..but it was what it all means I knew I hadn't got the full gist of it and I'm aware of that."

One of the biggest bugbears of traditional exams according to our students is that there are no opportunities to learn from mistakes or remedy perceived errors because there is so little feedback.

> "I hate the way you don't ever get your exam paper back, you just get a mark. Say an exam's six subjects in it, you might have got one 100% correct and one 10%, but you don't know which one!"

> "Seeing my mark doesn't tell me anything. I thought I knew the material better, so therefore I know I've got to do more. But it may be that my lack is in a very specific area. I don't know. I'm not sure whether to revise in just the same way as I did before. Now I only know something wasn't done as it should be, but I don't know what to do next time."

When talking about peer assessment, students became much more aware of what the assessment process entails.

> "I found it really interesting to have to sit down and think about it all from another point of view.....Peer assessment certainly did help me think about how to approach answering something like that in the future."

Students seemed to develop a better understanding of the validity of the assessment criteria by using peer assessment; it seemed to help them understand what is really needed to produce a good piece of work:

> "[Seeing different examples of work] I thought was really good because you could just have one essay in front of you and think 'Yeah, that's quite good', but you need something to compare it against. One of them went whoosh! Into the Stats, but it had no relevance to the question at all. Whilst the other one knew the Stats to actually answer the question, and to build up an argument."

> "A: It's got a much better structure, they've really thought about it
> B: But it's got no facts in it. You can't just say something and not back it up.
> A: It'd be better if it had some of the figures from the first essay.
> B: But it is good because it has an introduction and a conclusion.
> C: Yes, but it makes sweeping statements."

What do students think about peer assessment?

One of the big advantages, they suggested, of peer assessment, was that it helped them to really get in touch with the criteria being used. Whereas students said of their understanding of criteria in traditional assessment "I have no idea" or "I haven't a clue", those engaged in peer assessment said:

> "It improved my understanding of how judgements are made about my work, because before I thought I knew what constituted a good essay and a bad essay, and then I went into more detail."

> "It's a valuable experience to learn, I mean, it would benefit us if we know how they are marking us. We can look at those points and put them in."

> "It was quite good to go away and think to yourself 'Well, I should do this in my essay, I shouldn't do that'."

> "I thought about it a lot more. If I do an essay normally.... I just tend to do it. (Having the criteria) was good because I looked at them a lot, thinking, 'Now have I answered all the questions?' (ie addressed all of the criteria)"

> "As I went through it (peer assessing) I picked out the good points and the bad points, then I went through it again and made notes on what they'd included and I hadn't , then I tried to justify the mark I had given."

Students told us, though, that it is really important to provide practice at using criteria before the actual assessment opportunity:

> "I think we would have been in the dark when it comes to peer marking if we hadn't had that practice session."

Conversely, students who didn't really get to grips with the process found it baffling:

> "Grading is really hard, to know whether to give them a 2 or a 4 , I've no idea how you draw the line, I just know if something is good or not."

Some of our data gave valuable insights into some of the things that can go wrong with peer assessment. For example, it was made clear that tutors can't just expect students to grasp the meaning of criteria that are wrapped up in complex language:

> "I didn't understand half of the things we were meant to circle anyway. So basically what I put down for one I put down for them all. So I didn't mark properly at all."

> "I sat there with these numbers and in the end it became a bit random. Perhaps the tutor finds it easier to break it all down into sections, that's up to her. But I just get a general feeling that's all."

What do students think about peer assessment?

"I found it very difficult.... I know you've got all the criteria and that, but it makes it so difficult the way the person had written the essay was so different from mine, yet it is still answering the question."

Our work on innovative assessment will have value for students and staff at our university if the learning we have derived from it is converted into best practice in its implementation. We conclude here with some suggestions on using peer assessment based on what we have learned from the students and staff who contributed to our studies. To be effective, peer assessment must:

- be couched in language that is accessible to the students who will be using it in practice;
- provide opportunities for students involved to become fully cognisant with the criteria being used, with the chance to think them through and ask questions about them;
- offer opportunities for mark-free rehearsals in which students can gauge the standards that they are trying to achieve;
- enable students to build up their powers of meaningful evaluation of work by enabling them to see examples, good and bad, of work produced by other students;
- be demonstrably authentic, in that it assesses what it is stated that it assesses and perceived to be fair in the way in which it is implemented;
- be well organised and capable of dealing with hiccups and glitches in ways that do not disadvantage any students.

A peer assessment system that can do all this will be a powerful agency for student learning.

Publications

L McDowell, K Sambell & S Brown, 'But is it fair?' an exploratory study of student perceptions of the consequential validity of assessment *Studies in Educational Evaluation* (forthcoming, 1997)

L McDowell, Enabling student learning through innovative assessment pp 159-165 in G Wisker and S Brown (eds) *Enabling student learning: systems and strategies,* Kogan Page, 1996, 0 7494 1790 0

L McDowell, The impact of innovative assessment on student learning, *Innovation in Education and Training International*, 32(4), 1995, p 302-313

L McDowell & G Mowl, Innovative assessment: its impact on students p131-147 in Gibbs G (ed) *Improving student learning through assessment and evaluation,* OCSD, 1995.

Practical pointers on peer-assessment

Phil Race
University of Durham

The purposes of this chapter are as follows:
- to provide some answers to the question 'why use peer-assessment?'-,
- to illustrate some answers to 'what lends itself to peer-assessment?',
- to address some of your concerns about 'how can 1 use peer-assessment?';
- to explore how students can be involved in formulating peer-assessment criteria;
- to help you get started on using peer-assessment.

Some reasons for using peer-assessment

Students are doing it already

Students are continuously peer-assessing in fact. One of the most significant sources of answers to students' pervading question: "How am 1 doing?" is the feedback they get about their own learning achievements and performances by comparing with those of others. It is true that feedback from tutors is regarded as more-authoritative, but there is less such feedback available from tutors than from fellow learners. Setting up and facilitating peer-assessment therefore legitimises and makes respectable something that most students are already engaged in.

Students find out more about our assessment cultures

One of the biggest dangers with assessment is that students often don't really know how their assessment works. They often approach both exams and tutor-marked coursework like black holes that they might be sucked into! Getting involved in peer-assessment makes the assessment culture much more transparent, and students gain a better idea of exactly what will be expected of them in their efforts to demonstrate their achievement of the intended learning outcomes.

We can't do as much assessing as we used to do

With more students, heavier teaching loads, and shorter timescales (sometimes caused by moves to modularisation and semesterisation), the amount of assessment that lecturers can cope with is limited. While it is to be hoped that our assessment will still be valid, fair and reliable, it remains the case that the amount of feedback to students that lecturers can give is less per capita. Peer-assessment, when facilitated well, can be a vehicle for getting much more feedback to students.

Practical pointers on peer-assessment

Students learn more deeply when they have a sense of ownership of the agenda

When peer-assessment is employed using assessment criteria that are devised by the students themselves, the sense of ownership of the criteria helps them to apply their criteria much more objectively than when they are applying tutors' criteria to each others' work.

The act of assessing is one of the deepest learning experiences

Applying criteria to someone else's work is one of the most productive ways of developing and deepening understanding of the subject matter involved in the process. 'Measuring' or 'judging' are far more rigorous processes than simply reading, listening, or watching.

Peer-assessment allows students to learn from each others' successes

Students involved in peer-assessment can not fail to take notice of instances where the work they are assessing exceeds their own efforts. When this learning-from-each-other is legitimised and encouraged, students can benefit a great deal from the work of the most-able in the group.

Peer-assessment allows students to learn from each others' weaknesses

Students peer-assessing are likely to discover all sorts of mistakes that they did not make themselves. This can be really useful for them, as their awareness of 'what not to do' increases, and they become much less likely to fall into traps that might otherwise have caused them problems in their future work.

What lends itself to peer-assessment?

Peer assessment can be an invaluable means of involving students closely in their own and each others' learning. It is not a 'quick fix' solution to reduce staff marking time, as it is intensive in its use of tutor time at the briefing and development stages. It has high payoff in terms of improved learning. The following are some of the many areas where peer-assessment can produce excellent benefits.

Student presentations. Peer-assessment is particularly useful for the style and process dimensions of student presentations. It can also be used for the content side of presentations, when the topics are sufficiently shared so that students are well-informed enough to make judgements on the content of each others' presentations.

Reports. Peer-assessment helps to alert learners to good and bad practice in report-writing, and helps them develop awareness of the importance of structure, coherence and layout in reports. Peer-assessment can also help to train students in the particular styles and formats they need to be able to use in the discipline area they are learning.

Essay-plans. Peer-assessment of essay-plans can widen learners' horizons about different ways of brainstorming the content and structure of essays. It takes almost as much creative thinking to design the content of an essay-plan as it would to produce the final essay, so peer-assessing such plans helps students to cover a lot of sharing of ideas in a relatively short time.

Practical pointers on peer-assessment

Calculations. Peer-assessing correct answers is simple and quick. Peer-assessment allows students to identify exactly where things went wrong when marking incorrect answers, and alerts learners to potential trouble spots to avoid in the future.

Interviews. Peer-assessment allows students to exchange a range of opinions, attitudes and reactions to each others' interview performance, in a less threatening way than can be the case when such performance is tutor-assessed.

Annotated bibliographies. Peer-assessment of bibliographies can be a fast and effective way of alerting learners to other sources of reference, that learners working on their own might otherwise have overlooked.

Practical work. Peer-assessment of experimental work can allow learners to receive feedback on their practical skills, when tutor-assessment of such skills may be threatening - or not possible, for example due to limited tutor availability when large groups of students are involved.

Poster displays. Peer-assessment of poster-displays can be a rapid way of alerting learners to a wide range of approaches to the visual presentation of ideas. Especially when the peer-assessment of posters is done in a formative way (i.e. the results don't count towards an award), students can approach the task in a relaxed way, and exercise their individuality in interpreting each display using the criteria agreed. This can lead to useful class discussions about individuality, subjectivity, and originality.

Portfolios. Where students are familiar with all the requirements for the successful demonstration of their achievements through portfolios, students are often highly competent in assessing each others', particularly if they themselves have recently undertaken a similar preparation task.

Exhibitions and artifacts. Art and Design students in particular have a long tradition of participating in critiques of each others' paintings, plans, models, garments, sculptures and so on. Students participating in 'crits' learn a lot about the level of work required, and the ways in which aesthetic judgements of work are formed within their own particular subject contexts.

In all of the above instances, establishing the criteria is a crucial step. This is explored in some detail next.

Getting criteria from the students

As mentioned already, peer-assessment works at its best when students own the assessment criteria. Furthermore, it is important that the criteria are clearly understood by all the students, and their understanding is shared. The best way of developing a set of good criteria is to involve the students from the outset in the process. It is crucial not to put words in students' mouths during this process, otherwise the assessment agenda can revert to academic terminology which students don't understand. The following processes can be used to generate a set of peer-assessment criteria 'from scratch'. The author has used this process with groups of nearly 200 students, as well as with more-intimate groups of 20 upwards.

Practical pointers on peer-assessment

It really does not matter what the task that students are going to peer-assess involves. The process below will be described in terms of students peer-assessing 'a presentation', but the process could be identical for generating student-owned assessment criteria for an essay, a report, a poster display, an interview, an annotated bibliography, a student-devised exam paper, and countless other assessment possibilities.

It is possible to go through all of the processes listed below, with a group of over 100 students, in less than an hour. The more often you do this with students, the faster and better you and they will become at it (and at taking short-cuts where appropriate, or tailoring the steps to your own subject, and to the particular students, and so on. Some of the processes described in the list below may be skipped, but it is worth thinking through the implications of all of the stages before making your own decision about which are most relevant to the particular conditions under which you are planning to facilitate peer-assessment.

1. Ask all students to write down some key words about "what makes a really good 10-minute presentation? Jot down some of the things you would look for in an excellent example of one".

2. Get students to work in groups. Even in a large lecture theatre, they can work in groups of 4 or 5 with their near neighbours. Alternatively, if students are free to move around the room where the exercise is happening, they can be put into random groups (alphabetical, or by birthday month, or allowed to form self-selecting groups). Ask the groups to share and discuss for a few minutes all of their ideas for a good presentation.

3. Ask the groups to make a short list of (say) "The most important **five** features of a good 10-minute presentation". Ask each group to appoint a scribe to note down the short list.

4. Get the groups to look carefully at the wording of each item on their short lists. For example, tell them that when they report back an item from their list, if you can't tell exactly what it means, you will ask them to tell you "what it really means is........." Maybe mention that some of the more academic words such as 'coherence', 'structure' and 'delivery' may need some translation into everyday words (maybe along the lines of 'hangs well together, one point following on logically to the next...' , 'good interest-catching opening, logical order for the middle, and firm solid conclusion', and 'clearly-spoken, well-illustrated, backed-up by facts or figures....'). However, don't put too many words of any kind into students' minds, let them think of their own words.

5. Remind the groups about the short listing process, and to get their five features into order of priority.

6. Suggest that the groups now edit each of their features into a question-format. For example, "was there a good finish?", "How well was the material researched?" and so on. The point of this is to pave the way for a checklist of criteria that will be more-straightforward as a basis for making judgements.

Practical pointers on peer-assessment

7. Now start collecting 'top' feature-questions. Ask each group in turn for the thing that came top of its list. Write these up, one at a time, on a flip chart or overhead transparency, so that the whole class can see the emerging list of criteria. Where one group's highest-rating point is very similar to one that has already been given, either put a tick beside the original one (to acknowledge that the same point has been rated as important by more than one group), or (better) adjust the wording slightly so that the flip charted criterion reflects **both** of the sources equally. Continue this process until each of the groups has reported its top criterion.

8. Now go back round the groups (in reverse order) asking for "the second-most-important thing on your list". At this stage, the overlaps begin to occur thick and fast, but there will still emerge new and different checklist-questions based on further features identified by the groups. Use ticks (maybe in a different colour from the overlaps of top-rated questions) to make the degree of concurrence visible to the whole group as the picture continues to unfold. With a large class, you may need to use more than one flipchart-sheet (or overhead transparency), but it is important to try to keep all of the agenda that is unfolding visible to the whole class. This means posting up filled flipcharts where everyone can see them, or alternating the transparencies so that students remember what has already come up.

9. If the degree of overlap has increased significantly, and after gaining all the second-round contributions, the flow of new ideas has slowed down, it is worth asking the whole group for "any fairly-important things that still aren't represented on your list?". Usually, there will be a further two or three significant contributions at this stage.

10. When all of the criteria-questions have been noted down, **number them.** Simply write numbers beside each criterion, in the order that they were given. During this stage, if you notice that two criteria are more-or-less the same, it can be worth asking the class whether you can clump them together.

11. Ask students to work individually again next. Ask them to weight each criterion, using an agreed total number of marks. Choosing the total number needs care! If there are ten criteria, 100 marks would be too tempting regarding the possibility of some students just giving each criterion ten marks, and avoiding the real business of making prioritising decisions again. Thirteen criteria and sixty marks works better, for example. Ask every student to ensure that the total marks number adds up to the agreed figure. Legitimise students regarding ignoring any criteria that they individually don't think are important: "If you think it's irrelevant, just score it zero".

12. The next stage is to record everyone's marks on the flipcharts or transparencies. This means starting with criterion number 1, and writing beneath it **everyone's** marks-rating. It's worth establishing a reporting-back order round the room first, so that every student knows who to follow (and encouraging students to nudge any one who has lost concentration and is failing to give you a score!). "Can you shout them out as fast as 1 can write them up?" usually keeps everyone (including you) working at speed.

Practical pointers on peer-assessment

13. It can be worth starting with two flipcharts from the outset. For example, you may wish to record separately the criteria relating to **content** and those relating to **structure**. This may pave the way for peer-assessment grids which help to separate such dimensions.

14. Then go through all of the remaining criteria in the same way. Don't worry that sometimes consecutive scores for the same criterion will be quite divergent. When this happens, it will be a rich agenda for discussion later, and if you're writing the scores up in the same order each time, it's not too hard to pinpoint the particular individual who gave an unusually high or low rating to any criterion. You can, for example, ask the student who rated criterion 8 highest to argue briefly with the student who rated it lowest, and see what the causes of the divergence may be.

15. Next, average out all the scores. If there are students with calculators in the group, the average rating may be forthcoming from the group without any prompting. Otherwise, it's usually possible to do some averaging and rounding up or down to the nearest whole number just intuitively by looking at the numbers. Ask the whole group "Does criterion 7 get a 5 or a 6 please? Hands up those who make it a 5?" and so on.

16. Look back at the whole range of criteria and ratings. At this point, there will usually be one or more criteria that can safely be dropped from the agenda. They may have seemed like a good idea at the time to some of the students, but the visible ratings tell their own story.

17. "Are you all happy to proceed with the averaged-out version of the ratings, and with these criteria?" is the question to ask next. Mostly, there will be no dissent. Just occasionally, a student with a different view of the ratings may wish to speak out against the consensus. It is worth then offering any individuals who feel strongly about the ratings can choose to be peer-assessed by their own idiosyncratic rating scales, but that these must now be shared with the whole group for approval. Students rarely wish to do this, particularly if the feeling of ownership of the set of weighted criteria is strong in the group as a whole.

18. Turn the criteria-questions into a grid, with the criteria down the left-hand-side, and the weighting numbers in a column alongside them, with spaces for students to write in their peer-assessment ratings. If students are going to be asked to peer-assess several instances of the task involved (for example maybe 10 short presentations) the grids could be marked up so that students used the same grid for the successive presentations (see Figure 1). Alternatively, if the peer-assessment grids are going to be used for a small number of assessments (for example, where all students mark three essays or reports, and each of theirs is to be marked by three students), it is worth having separate sheets, with a column for individual feedback comments relating to the score awarded for each of the criteria (see Figure 2).

The list of processes above may appear daunting, but in fact it is quite a lot easier to do in practice than it is to write out a description of it! Also, some of the steps are in fact very quick to do. Furthermore, as the culture of peer-assessment becomes better known to students, they themselves become better at generating and weighting criteria, and more-skilled at applying them well.

Peer-assessment grid

Your name: **Date:**   **Session:**

Example being assessed:	Mark:	A	B	C	D	E	F	G	H
Criterion 1	6								
Criterion 2	8								
Criterion 3	4								
Criterion 4	8								
Criterion 5	5								
Criterion 6	5								
Criterion 7	2								
Criterion 8	4								
Total	**42**								

Figure 1: *example of a grid where students peer-assess A to H (for example) presentations*

Peer-assessment grid

Your name: **Date:**   **Session:**

Example being assessed:	Mark:	score	Feedback comments
Criterion 1	6		
Criterion 2	8		
Criterion 3	4		
Criterion 4	8		
Criterion 5	5		
Criterion 6	5		
Criterion 7	2		
Criterion 8	4		
Total	**42**	**40**	

Figure 2: *Pro-forma for individual peer-assessments of (for example) essays or reports, with feedback*

Some suggestions for getting the most from peer-assessment

Increasingly peer-assessment is being used to involve students more closely in their learning and its evaluation, and to help to enable students really understand what is required of them. It can have enormous benefits in terms of learning gain, but is not to be regarded as a short-cut to tutors wishing to lighten their assessment burden. Setting up peer-assessment may well involve greater effort from tutors in the early stages, although long term there will be savings in tutor time. The following suggestions may help you get started with student peer-assessment.

Take it a bit at a time.
Some people (students and tutors) find the use of peer-assessment is very radical, so it is a good idea to introduce it gradually, on a small scale, until you, your colleagues and students are confident about how it will work best. It is best to gain some experience using peer-assessment under conditions where the purposes are purely formative, before venturing into using it for assessments which count towards an award.

Keep everyone in the picture.
Tell everyone what you are doing and why. Students and colleagues need to understand the thinking behind what you are doing, to avoid them perceiving it as a soft option or abdication of responsibility. If students understand that peer-assessment is actually intended to significantly deepen their learning processes, they may find it more acceptable.

Provide mark-free rehearsal opportunities.
This helps students get the hang of what is required of them, and also builds in an opportunity for students to get interim feedback at a stage where there is time to bring about improvements. Particularly for students who are going to be involved in peer-assessment which counts towards an award, it is vital for them to have sufficient practice so that they can find out how to participate effectively.

Provide, or negotiate, really-clear assessment criteria.
Students should not be able to over-mark friends or penalise enemies if the criteria are unambiguous and explicit. All marks should be justifiable by reference to the criteria, and to the evidence of achievement of them. It can help to hold class discussion of the evidence which will be acceptable to prove that each assessment criterion has been achieved, and the different standards of evidence that will lead to different scores or grades.

Make peer-assessment marks meaningful.
Some argue that peer review is really only suitable for feedback purposes. However, if students are to take peer-assessment seriously, it should count for something, even if it is only a small proportion of the final grade. You may prefer to parallel-mark, with tutor grades counting as well as averaged peer-grades if this is appropriate.

Moderate peer assessment.
To ensure that the students see peer-assessment as fair, tutors must overview the marks awarded and provide a 'court of appeal' if students feel justice has not been done. This may mean offering vivas to any dissatisfied candidates.

Keep the system simple.
Try not to give yourself really complicated addition and averaging tasks to do after peer assessment has taken place. Too many separate components make it laborious to arrive at final marks. If the numerical side can't be simplified, it is worth using computer programs to do the donkey work!

Involve students in the assessment criteria. As has been shown in some detail earlier in this chapter, you can do this by letting students participate in the generation of assessment criteria, and the weighting to be given to each criterion. Alternatively, you can provide the criteria in the first instance, and give students lots of opportunities to ask questions about what they really mean.

Allow plenty of time.
Just because **you** can assess a poster display or an essay fairly quickly doesn't mean that students will be able to do so too, especially if groups are assessing other groups and are required to provide a mark by consensus. Presentations **always** over-run, and students will tend to make snap conclusions and 'guesstimates' when under pressure regarding time.

Monitor student achievement.
It's a good idea to review how well students are peer-assessing, by the same kinds of methods you may use to review your own assessment, to ensure reliability and validity of marking. It is often reassuring for students (and colleagues) to see that peer-assessment using explicit criteria, and based on the production of clearly specified evidence, produces data that are very similar to marks produced by tutors themselves.

Some further reading

There is a wide-ranging literature on assessment. The sources below may help both to explore further some of the benefits (and limitations) of peer-assessment, and to set peer-assessment appropriately in the wider scheme of assessment in your institution.

Andressen, L, Nightingale, P, Boud, D and Magin, D (1989) Strategies for Assessing Students - *Teaching with Reduced Resources* SEDA Paper 78,Birmingham,UK

Atkins, M J, Beattie, W B and Dockerell (1993) *Assessment Issues in Higher Education* Department of Employment, London

Baume, C and Baume D (1986) *Learner Know Thyself - Self-Assessment and Self-Determining Assessing in Education* The New Era **67** 3 5-67

Bell, C and Harris, D (1994) *Evaluating and Assessing for Learning (2nd Revised Edition)* Kogan Page London

Practical pointers on peer-assessment

Brown, S and Knight, P (1994) *Assessing Learners in Higher Education* Kogan Page, London

Brown, S and Race, P (1994) *Assess Your Own Teaching Quality* Kogan Page, London

Brown, S, Race, P and Smith, B (1995) 500 *Tips on Assessment* Kogan Page, London.

Brown, S, Rust, C and Gibbs, G (1994) *Strategies for Diversifying Assessment in Higher Education* Oxford Centre for Staff Development, Oxford Brookes University, UK

Conway, R et al (1993) *Peer Assessment of an Individual's Contribution to a Group Project Assessment and Evaluation in Higher Education*, 18 1 45-56

Knight,P(ed)(1995) *Assessment for Learning in Higher Education* Kogan Page SEDA Series, London

Race, P (1993) *Never Mind the Teaching, Feel the Learning* SEDA Paper 80, Birmingham, UK

Rowntree D (1989) *Assessing Students: How Shall we Know Them?* (2nd Revised Edition) Kogan Page, London

Rust, R and Wallace, J (1994) *Helping Students to Learn From Each Other* SEDA Paper 86, Birmingham, UK